MASONIC REPRINTS

AND

HISTORICAL REVELATIONS,

INCLUDING

Original Notes and Additions,

BY

HENRY SADLER, P.M. & P.Z.,

Grand Tyler & Sub-Librarian of the Grand Lodge of England.

AUTHOR OF "MASONIC FACTS AND FICTIONS," "THOMAS DUNCKERLEY," &c.

AND AN INTRODUCTORY CHAPTER

BY

W. J. CHETWODE CRAWLEY, LL.D., D.C.L.,

Past Senior Grand Deacon, Ireland, &c., &c.

—

History is Philosophy teaching by examples.—*Bolingbroke.*

—

GEORGE KENNING,
16 AND 16A, GREAT QUEEN STREET. LONDON, W.C.
—
1898.

The Erroneous Pagination Appears As It Was In The Original Book.

To

The Worshipful Brother,

Witham Matthew Bywater,

Past Master of the Royal Athelstan Lodge, No. 19,

and the Quatuor Coronati Lodge, No. 2076,

Past Grand Sword Bearer

of the

United Grand Lodge of Free and Accepted

Masons of England,

In Appreciation of his Masonic Virtues,

and in acknowledgment of his Literary efforts

on behalf of

Laurence Dermott

and other Brethren of Antient Origin,

This Volume

is

Respectfully and Fraternally Dedicated.

London, 1898.

CONTENTS.

PREFACE.

The exhaustive and scholarly contribution from the pen of Dr. Chetwode Crawley has, in my opinion, rendered prefatory remarks on the contents of this book almost unnecessary. I shall therefore avail myself of the present opportunity for placing on record my gratitude and high appreciation of his great personal kindness on this as well as on many previous occasions, and his readiness at all times to assist in elucidating the more obscure periods of the history of our Order, especially such as relate to early Freemasonry in Ireland. Anything approaching to adulation would, I am sure, be as repugnant to him as to myself; but I cannot do less than express a firm conviction that his Introductory Chapter forms, by far, the most important portion of the volume, and that this conviction will be shared by Masonic students generally. In order, however, that its value may be appreciated by those who are not acquainted with the early history of the Craft, I have deemed it advisable to reproduce, without comment, some of the known references to Speculative Masonry in England anterior to 1688, the date of the manuscript Dr. Chetwode Crawley has so opportunely discovered.

For the sake of completeness, I preface what Dr. Chetwode Crawley terms the public notices of the Craft, with extracts from the Minute-books of the Masons' Company and the old Lodge at Edinburgh.

The Records of the Masons' Company of London for the year 1620 contain the following :—

"They charge themselves also wth money receyved of the Psns hereafter named for their gratuitie at theyr acceptance unto the Livery, viz." Here follow six names and payments.

Under dates 1621 and 1631 are entries which seem to indicate still more clearly the existence of Speculative Masonry :—

"Att the making masons, viz., John Hince, John Brown, Rowland Everett, Evan Lloyd, James ffrench, John Clarke, Thomas Rose, reced of them as appear^tb by the quart^h. booke."

1631. "Paid in goeing abroad and att a meeting att the Hall about the Masons that were to be accepted, 6s. 6d."[1]

The minute-book of the Lodge of Edinburgh (Mary's Chapel) No. 1 contains a record of the admission at Newcastle, on the 20th May, 1641, of "Mr. Robert Moray, General quarterm^r. to the Armie off Scotlan."[2]

Ashmole's Diary, Oct. 16th, 1646 :

"I was made a Free Mason
at Warrington in Lancashire, with Coll: Henry
Mainwaring of Karincham in Cheshire.
The names of those that were then of the Lodge;
Mr Rich Penket Warden, Mr James Collier, Mr Rich:
Sankey, Henry Littler, John Ellam, Rich: Ellam
& Hugh Brewer."

---

[1] "Records of the Hole Crafte and Fellowship of Masons." Edward Conder, Junior. London, 1894.

[2] "History of the Lodge of Edinburgh." David Murray Lyon Edinburgh, 1873.

Ibid, March 10th, 1682:

"I rec^d a Summons to appe at a Lodge to be held the next day, at Masons Hall London. Accordingly I went, & about Noone were admitted into the Fellowship of Free Masons, Sr William Wilson Knight, Capt. Rich: Borthwick, Mr Will: Woodman, Mr Wm Grey, Mr Samuell Taylour & Mr William Wise. I was the Senior Fellow among them (it being 35 yeares since I was admitted) There were p^esent beside my selfe the Fellowes after named.

Mr Tho: Wise M^r of the Masons Company this p^esent yeare. Mr Thomas Shorthose, Mr Thomas Shadbolt,   Waindsford Esqr Mr Nich: Young. Mr John Shorthose, Mr William Hamon, Mr John Thompson, & Mr Will: Stanton.

Wee all dyned at the halfe Moone Taverne in Cheapeside, at a Noble Dinner prepaired at the charge of the New-accepted Masons." [1]

The oft-quoted Dr. Plot, in 1686, says: "To these add the *Customs* relating to the *County*, whereof they have one, of admitting men into the *Society* of *Free-Masons*, that in the *moorelands* of this *County* seems to be of greater request, than anywhere else, though I find the *Custom* spread more or less all over the *Nation;* for here I found persons of the most eminent quality, that did not disdain to be of this *Fellowship.* . . . .

. . . . Into which Society when they are admitted they call a *meeting* (or *Lodg* as they term it in some places) which must consist at lest of 5 or 6 of the Ancients of the *Order*, whom the *candidats* present with

---

1. W. J. Chetwode Crawley, "Transactions of The Quatuor Coronati Lodge." Vol. XI., Part I. 1898.

gloves, and so likewise to their *wives*, and entertain with a *collation* according to the Custom of the place : This ended, they proceed to the *admission* of them, which chiefly consists in the communication of certain *secret signes*, whereby they are known to one another all over the *Nation.*"[1]

Under the heading of "Masons' Tools" Randle Holme, Herald and Antiquary, says: "I cannot but Honor the Fellowship of the Masons because of it Antiquity; and the more as being a Member of that Society, called Free - Masons. In being conversant amongst them I have observed the use of these severall Tools following, some wherof I have seen born in coats Armour."[2]

Much valuable and interesting matter relative to Randle Holme and Freemasonry at Chester in the 17th Century, will be found in a paper by W. Harry Rylands, F.S.A., published in the *Masonic Magazine*, Vol. IX. London, 1882.

Here, then, is reliable evidence of the existence of what we may fairly assume to have been a system of Speculative Masonry in England and, by inference, in Scotland, during several distinct periods of the 17th century. I have reasons for thinking that a kindred system was not unknown in Wales either during the closing years of the 17th century or the early part of the 18th, but although I have long been of opinion that the real history of early Speculative Masonry in Ireland was, as it were, "a sealed book," I had not the faintest

[1] "The Natural History of Stafford-Shire." Robert Plot, LL.D. Oxford, 1686.

[2] "The Academy of Armory and Blazon." Randle Holme. Chester, 1688.

idea that anything of the kind was ever practised there prior to the formation of the Grand Lodge of England in 1717.

I tender my sincere thanks to Br. William James Hughan for his courteous and ready responses to the several enquiries I have had occasion to make of him during the compilation of this, as well as my previous publications.

And, lastly, I gratefully acknowledge, on behalf of Dr. Chetwode Crawley as well as on my own behalf, the kindness of Br. Witham Matthew Bywater in accepting the dedication of this small volume. Our reasons for asking him to do us this honour is that we believe he was the first of the present generation of Masons to put pen to paper in defence of Laurence Dermott and his associates, and thus direct our thoughts to the same subject.

HENRY SADLER.

INTRODUCTORY CHAPTER

BY

W. J. CHETWODE CRAWLEY.

———◆———

EARLY IRISH FREEMASONRY

AND

DEAN SWIFT'S CONNECTION WITH
THE CRAFT.

════════════

TEN years have passed since Bro. Henry Sadler, in his "Masonic Facts and Fictions," demonstrated the true origin of the Grand Lodge of the Antients, and showed its close connection with Irish Freemasonry. The pamphlets and documents reproduced in the present volume bear on that connection. Indeed, the first pamphlet is the work of an eminent Irishman, now proved to have been a member of a London Lodge, and much of our Introduction must be taken up with showing how it came to pass that he, like so many other Irish magnates of that day, was an English Freemason.

Ignorance of the social conditions that made the Freemasonry of England one with that of Ireland formed not the least of the obstacles to the acceptance of Bro. Henry Sadler's theory. It is expedient, therefore, to recapitulate the conditions that made such homogeneity natural and inevitable.

A

All Freemasonry in existence to-day can be traced, through one channel or another, to the Grand Lodge of England. This general statement is particularly true of Ireland. The Freemasonry of Ireland in the days immediately succeeding the erection of the Grand Lodge for London and Westminster seems rather a part than a counterpart of the new system. In less than eight years from the foundation of the Premier Grand Lodge, the Sister Grand Lodge of Ireland stands forth as the compeer of the Grand Lodge of England, to which alone it owes precedence.

Many things wrought together to this end. There never had been any Freemasonry in Ireland, save that of England. To put it shortly, there were no edifices in Celtic Ireland calling for skilled labour. The Celts never took kindly to building. The ecclesiastical edifices, in which so much learning is said to have been preserved, seem to have been, for the most part, mere wattled booths. The Royal palaces, in which so much wealth is said to have been displayed, were little better than one-storyed huts. The Round towers seem of extreme antiquity, only in consequence of the crudeness of their construction. It may well be doubted whether there existed in the whole of Celtic Ireland any building, church, abbey, castle, or palace, which could find occupation for a Masons' lodge. The native annalists record innumerable instances of the assault and capture of duns and raths, hardly to be distinguished from Maori *pahs*. They never record the set siege of an embattled stone fortress, or even of a walled city, unless it be in Scandinavian hands.

We have to await the advent of the Anglo-Normans before we can find edifices that will justify us in ascribing their erection to the skilled Brotherhood of Masons. The historian of Mediæval Freemasonry in Ireland is not called upon to decide between the claims of the Freemasons who built cathedrals and the Masons who belonged to the Guild. There was no Guild of Masons in Ireland, although there were in Dublin Guilds or Companies, counterparts of almost all the other Guilds or Companies that existed in London. The organization of Freemasons in England included Ireland in its jurisdiction. The cathedrals of Dublin were built by bands or lodges of Ecclesiastical Masons who came here from English centres, and who went away when it suited them. The sources whence they came are known. The national cathedral of St. Patrick, in Dublin, was begun under the auspices of Archbishop Henry de Londres, who brought over his company of London Masons that had been engaged in building the church of St. Mary Overie, Southwark. The diocesan cathedral of the Holy Trinity, now called Christ Church, Dublin, was built by successive companies or lodges of Masons, of which one at least was a swarm from the hive that built the cathedral at Wells, in Somerset. And so of other ecclesiastical edifices in Ireland. The London Guild of Masons seems to have had no influence on our architecture, whatever it may have had on our tradesmen.

It must be remembered that Dublin was never a Celtic city. The Ostmen founded it, and the Ostmen held it till the Anglo-Normans put an end to the Scandinavian kingdom of Dublin. From the date of seizure by the Anglo-Normans, extreme pains were taken to keep it free from Celtic admixture. The citizens of Dublin regarded themselves not as Irish, but as Englishmen settled in Ireland. No more strenuous supporter of this claim can be found than Dean Swift, who never wearied of insisting on the right of himself and his fellows to be regarded as English. The thoughts current in Dublin were the thoughts current across the Channel. The social institutions of Dublin were the social institutions of London, as near as might be. The space in Dublin was narrower, hence social enthusiasms ran all the higher. The features inherited by the Speculative Lodges from their Operative forefathers grew, if anything, more marked in Dublin. The characteristics of Modern Freemasonry that strike outsiders are the private means of recognition, the wide area from which fit candidates

A I

are selected, and the practical goodwill of the Brethren towards one another. We shall presently show that these were the characteristics that struck an intelligent onlooker in Dublin while the Stuart dynasty still held the throne, and that they were then taken as the publicly recognised marks of the Craft.

When the tide of Freemasonry, overspreading its former ebb with its new influx, absorbed the lodges of London and Westminster, its waves flowed into the English cities that happened to lie in Ireland. We find the same men at the head of the Fraternity on both sides of the Channel.

In 1725, Sir Thomas Prendergast is Senior Grand Warden of Ireland and Junior Grand Warden of England at the same time. In 1729-30, Lord Kingston earns the title of International Grand Master by serving the office in both countries. In 1733 Lord Southwell, who had served as Grand Master of Ireland before 1730, presides in the Grand Lodge of England by virtue of his past rank.

The Hon. James O'Brien and Springett Penn, respectively Grand Master and Deputy Grand Master of Munster before 1730, were members of London lodges. In 1723, an astute bookseller's hack thought it worth while to recommend his pamphlet by dedicating it "To the Grand Master, Masters, Wardens, and Brethren of the Most Antient and Most Honourable Fraternity of the Free Masons of Great Britain and Ireland." When the growing popularity of the revived Craft excited curiosity about its secret rites, the first of the Spurious Rituals was published in 1724. The attack in London drew forth a reply from Dublin. The scribes saw no difference between the systems.

If these facts had been known, or, being known, had been properly appreciated, the reception given to Bro. Henry Sadler's "Masonic Facts and Fictions" would have been greatly modified. It would have been seen that English and Irish Freemasonry continued to be convertible terms for the first ten or twelve years after the revival.

It would have been seen how naturally the English development after 1730 began to differ from the system common to both countries before 1730. It would have been seen, too, how Irish brethren, imbued with the more archaic Ritual, could not but look askance on the " variations and additions" that met them when they crossed to England. But none of these things were seen at the time ; indeed, most of the historical facts set forth above have been put in their proper relation to the history of Freemasonry only since the publication of Bro. Henry Sadler's "Masonic Facts and Fictions."

The foremost literary men of the Augustan age that saw the foundation of the Grand Lodges of England and Ireland were almost as familiar figures in the society of Dublin as in that of London. Swift, Addison, Tickell, Parnell, Steele, had all been residents of Dublin, and with them were closely linked Pope, Arbuthnot, Gay, and the whole galaxy of that Augustan age. The revival of Freemasonry was as striking on one side of the Channel as on the other, and could no more escape the notice of Swift in Dublin than of Pope in London. It would be natural to expect that if some of these great names should be shown to belong to Freemasons, others of their associates would be found in the ranks of the Craft. This is precisely what has been ascertained by the intelligent and well-directed researches of Bro. Henry Sadler.

The difficulties in the way are considerable. The sources of information are incomplete, and the indications are obscure. It is precisely in such cases that the skill of the trained observer is invaluable.

Although the present enquiry has to do with the reception into the Craft of that most eminent Irishman, Dean Swift, the sources of information are practically confined to the English records. We have elsewhere told the story of the lost archives of the Grand Lodge of Ireland. We have even shown that the official History, published by the Grand Secretary of Ireland in 1751, ignores the doings of his Grand Lodge before 1730, as completely as if such a body had never existed. We are, therefore, dependent on the MS. Lists of individual members of lodges preserved in the archives, so zealously guarded by Bro. Henry Sadler.

As far as the period with which we have to deal is concerned, there exist three Grand Lodge Registers, or lists of members, covering the years from 1723 to 1733. Each of these lists was separately made, and appears to have been intended as an official return to the Grand Secretary. They are well known to students as the First (or 1723) List ; the Second (or 1725) List ; and the Third (or 1730) List.

The First of these Lists was begun on 25th November, 1723, and probably includes members returned in the early months of 1724. It enumerates 52 lodges, but only 36 of these have the return of members' names appended.

The Second List was begun two years later, 27th November, 1725. Like the First, it evidently included the names of members admitted during the year following its nominal date, or even later. Some of the more recent lodges in the list must have made their returns in 1727 and 1728. This is by far the most complete of the three lists, as only 4 out of the 77 lodges enumerated lack the members' names.

The Third (or 1730) List is the least satisfactory of the three. Unfortunately, it seems to add inexactness of transcription to incompleteness of enumeration. It was originally intended to include the members of the various lodges who had been made, or who had joined since the preceding return. This list would be more properly ascribed to 1731 or 1732. It even includes certain of the later lodges constituted in 1733. Nevertheless, barely one half of the 102 lodges enumerated have lists of names appended, 47 being left totally blank. It is not easy to determine, at this distance of time, whether these blanks were caused by the lodges failing to make returns, or are owing to remissness on the part of the clerk. Something is probably due to the latter cause. The entries compare unfavourably with those in the former registers, either as to accuracy of nomenclature, or as to correctness of orthography. So marked is this difference that Bro. Henry Sadler has come to the conclusion that the 1723 and 1725 lists were written in the register by the Grand Secretary himself, while the 1730 list was written by a clerk, or scrivener, who evidently knew little or nothing about the identity of the people whose names he was copying. Many of the names correctly entered in the previous lists are wrongly spelled by the uninterested or unintelligent clerk who copied out the 1730 list. It is important to bear in mind the shortcomings of the clerk, because a mis-rendering of Jon. Swift's Christian name and style has obscured his identification. *

Such are the materials on which we have to work. It will be observed that no argument can be drawn from the inadequate description of a member, or even the entire absence of a name. The gaps are too wide and too frequent. This is especially true of the Third (or 1730) Register, in which we seem to suffer more from clerical shortcomings than in either of the others. In any case, we would do well to remember that, during the period covered by these lists, there were numbers of legitimate Freemasons whose names could not appear on any such register. These Brethren were not irregular or clandestine. They were only Non-Regular in that they had not yet agreed to place themselves under the jurisdiction (*sub regulâ*) of the newly-formed Grand Lodges of England and Ireland. There were no other Grand Lodges then in existence, for the Grand Lodge of Scotland belongs to the next decade.

---

* These Lists have been discussed by Bro. John Lane, F.C.A, ("Handy Book of the Lists of Lodges"; Kenning, London, 1889). from a different point of view, as bearing on the succession of Lodges, not on the identification of the members.

Throughout our Augustan age there existed a particular literary coterie, in which the rivalry of genius proved no bar to constancy of friendship. Following out our previous train of thought, if any one member of it should be found amongst our Fraternity, we should look to find other members there too. The leading members of this coterie were John Arbuthnot (1675-1735), Alex. Pope (1688-1744), and Jon. Swift (1667-1745). Of this trio Bishop Warburton says : " Arbuthnot was skilled in everything related to science ; Pope was a master in the fine arts ; and Swift excelled in a knowledge of the world. Wit they had all in equal measure, and this so large that no age, perhaps, ever produced three men to whom nature had more bountifully bestowed it, or art had brought it to higher perfection."

They had been bound together for many years by the closest political and intellectual ties. They had formed in 1714 the Martinus Scriblerus Club, and pointedly addressed each other as Brother. Here, then, was the quarry for Bro. Henry Sadler's sagacious research to track down. All three turned out to be members of our Craft Nay, the Dean of St. Patrick's, at first sight the least likely of the three, turns out to have used his pen in defence of his brethren, or, at least, in reprobation of the Spurious Rituals foisted on an undiscriminating public.

The first of the coterie to join the Craft seems to have been Dr. John Arbuthnot, M.D. of the University of Aberdeen. The same ancient seat of learning had been the *Alma Mater* of the Rev. James Anderson, M.A.—a circumstance probably not without its bearing on the matter in hand. This Scottish physician practised in London with a professional success rarely attained by a man of his eminence as a wit and an author. Arbuthnot, not inferior to his colleagues in solid learning or polite taste, was superior to them in the great gift of genial humour. It is he who has affixed for all time to the honest, plodding Englishman the nickname of John Bull. By this, if by nothing else, he has achieved immortality.

The name of this kindly Scot is entered in the list of 1725, and is on the roll of members of the lodge held at the Bedford Head, Covent Garden. This hostelry gave its name and shelter to a flourishing lodge of 41 members, all apparently men of good social standing. Martin Folkes, a distinguished Freemason, was on its roll. There were, besides, seven styled Esquire, four Doctors, two with the prefix Hon., two with the prefix Sir, and two styled Reverend. In such company, Dr. Arbuthnot found himself among associates to his liking.*

---

* Though less known than his compeers to the ordinary English reader, Dr. Arbuthnot was excelled by no man of his day, not even by Swift himself, in the art of fitly expressing condensed thought. This exquisite art is the special attribute of the Greek and Roman writers. If one were asked to supply to an English reader a specimen of the peculiar power of style that forms the perennial charm of the classical writers. no better example could be chosen than the following epitaph—the most tremendous in the English language—in which Arbuthnot has gibbeted, for all time, the notorious Colonel Chartres, who, after a long life of villainy, was charged with the capital crime of an attempted outrage on his servant-maid :

" Here continueth to rot the body of FRANCIS CHARTRES, who, with an inflexible constancy and inimitable uniformity of life, persisted, in spite of age and infirmities, in the practice of every human vice. excepting prodigality and hypocrisy ; his insatiable avarice exempted him from the first. his matchless impudence from the second. Nor was he more singular in the undeviating pravity of his manners, than successful in accumulating wealth : for, without trade or profession, without trust of public money, and without bribeworthy service, he acquired, or more properly created, a ministerial estate. He was the only person of his time who could cheat without the mask of honesty ; retain his primæval meanness when possessed of ten thousand a year ; and, having daily deserved the gibbet for what he did, was at last condemned to it for what he could not do.

" O indignant reader ! Think not his life useless to mankind ! Providence connived at his execrable designs, to give to after ages conspicuous proof and example of how small estimation is exorbitant wealth in the sight of God, by his bestowing it on the most unworthy of all mortals."

The foregoing has been printed as continuous prose in order to do away with the glamour of the broken lines in which it was originally couched, after the manner of monumental inscriptions. Divested of funeral trappings, the serried march of the words, keeping time with the thoughts, and all compressed within the compass of a few lines, will give the English reader an idea of what is meant by a classic style.

It seems a fair argument that, as Arbuthnot was a
Freemason, his lifelong intimates would, sooner or later,
be found to have joined the Craft.   Consequently, Bro.
Henry Sadler was led to search for and detect the names
of Pope and Swift, not, indeed, in the list of 1725, but
in that of 1730.   We have already seen the defects of
this list, and neither name escapes scot free.   But when
the deficiencies are so manifold, we may be thankful
that the names occur in such a way as to be at all recog-
nisable.   They are on the roll of the lodge held at the
" Goat at foot of the Haymarket."   All the members,
no matter what their calling, are entered with the prefix
Mr., with the exception of one gentleman of unmis-
takeable Irish patronymic, " Ger. [ald.?] Rorke, Esq."
Consequently, both names are somewhat disguised, the
great poet appearing as Mr. Alex. Pope, and the great
satirist as Mr. John Swift.

At first sight, the identification of the latter name
with that of Jonathan Swift, D.D., would seem
doubtful, but a little consideration will show so many
circumstances in its favour as to invest the case with
that highest kind of probability which we call moral
certainty, and which falls short of legal certainty only
through deficiency of technically legal evidence.   At
this very time—1726 and 1727—Swift was in London,
the guest of Pope at Twickenham. " Gulliver's Travels "
had just been published, and at once attained unbounded
popularity.   He sunned himself in the society of
Arbuthnot and Pope, and shared with them all the
convivialities of London, from which he had been so
long absent.   If they took part in Freemasonry, we may
be sure he joined them.   And there is no doubt about
Arbuthnot or Pope.   To make his connection with
Freemasonry doubly sure, Swift, as we have already had
occasion to indicate, took on himself the defence of the
Craft by a *reductio ad absurdum* of the Spurious Rituals
then current in London.   The solemn-faced travesty
forms the first of the literary curiosities which Bro.
Henry Sadler reproduces in this volume.   The perversion

of Swift's Christian name into John would naturally arise from his not unusual signature Jon. Swift, an obvious trap for a careless clerk.

(SIGNATURE OF DEAN SWIFT, 1732.)

The clerk has thrown an additional difficulty in our way by omitting Swift's ecclesiastical designation. But in this, he served Swift no worse than he served other clergymen. For instance, he describes as " Mr. John Savage," without the least hint of clerical qualification, the Rev. Dr. Savage, of St. George's, Hanover-square, a divine and scholar whose memory is yet green at Westminster School, and who had the honour of being a member along with Swift in the lodge held at the Goat. It is to be regretted that the form of registration supplies only the bare fact of membership at the date of making the return. It would be a matter of much interest to learn when and how such Brethren joined the Craft.*

These indications fit together so closely, and point so uniformly in the same direction, that we can conclude, with such reasonable certainty as guides men in the conduct of their daily life, that Dr. John Arbuthnot, Alexander Pope, and Dean Swift, were bound together

---

* It would be equally interesting to learn whether " Mr. William Smith," whose name immediately precedes that of " Mr. John Savage " on the roll, was that Bro. William Smith who compiled the " Free Mason's Pocket Companion," 1735, and was the first to publish, under the sanction of the Grand Lodge of Ireland, the world-wide " Entered Apprentice's Charge."

by the ties of our Brotherhood, in like manner as they were linked together throughout their lives by the ties of unswerving friendship.*

Allusions to Freemasonry are very rare in the literature of Swift's time. No mention of it has been traced in the letters that passed between Pope, Swift, and Arbuthnot. Pope has made incidental mention of it in "The Dunciad";—

> Some deep Freemasons join the silent race,
> Worthy to fill Pythagoras's place.
>
> BOOK iv., lines 572-573.

The Chevalier Andrew Ramsay, whose name is so prominent in Continental Freemasonry, was in correspondence with Swift in 1727-8, and again 1737-8; but the letters are formal in expression, and treat of matters purely literary. Nor is there any trace of Freemasonry in the intercourse between Swift and Philip, Duke of Wharton, whose acquaintance the Dean made in 1718, when he was admitted, though under age, to a seat (not to a vote) in the Irish House of Lords, in virtue of his Irish title of Marquis of Catherlough. The anecdote runs that when the Duke was parading in conversation some of his frolics, as he was pleased to call them, the Dean silenced the hereditary profligate with the sharp rebuke: "Aye, my Lord, let me recommend one more to you; pray take a frolic to be virtuous; it will do you more honour than all the rest." But this anecdote refers to the time of Wharton's visit to the Irish Metropolis, years before he posed as a Freemason.

So much for the notices of Freemasonry in Swift's later literary career. There exists, however, a notice of Freemasonry connected with his University days, so remarkable that it cannot be passed over. In the Universities of Oxford, Cambridge, and Dublin a custom

---

* Students conversant with the minuter details of our Augustan age will recall at least one other individual named Alexander Pope. This obscure namesake of the poet was unconnected with the literary triumvirate, and is, consequently, excluded by the tenour of the foregoing argument.—See Courthope's, and Carruthers' "Life of Pope," &c.

obtained during the seventeenth century of allowing a representative of the undergraduates to make a satirical speech at the annual meeting for conferring Degrees. The representative was called *Terrae Filius*, or Son of the Soil, and was granted full licence to air the grievances of his fellows, and to inveigh in unmeasured terms against anybody or anything that might excite their wrath. In Trinity College, Dublin, the ceremony of graduation was called Initia, or Commencements, and this particular part of it the Tripos. The Library of Trinity College possesses among its less known MSS. a copy of the Tripos of Midsummer, 1688, which was discovered and published by Dr. Barrett in 1808.* The *Terrae Filius* of that occasion was John Jones, a Scholar of the House, who outdid the ribaldry of his predecessors in a piebald compost of dog-Latin and bog-English. Dr. Barrett wasted a world of pains in trying to show that Swift wrote the speech, but succeeded only in showing that Swift and Jones were close friends. The Tripos contains notable—we had almost written astonishing — evidence concerning Freemasonry in Dublin in 1688.

We must premise that the circumstances and the personages mentioned in the Tripos have been shown to be connected with the University life of that day, though they have long passed into oblivion. The episode about Ridley or Ridlaeus is curious and puzzling. All we know of this worthy is summed up in Dr. Barrett's statement that he is reputed to have been an informer against priests under the barbarous Penal Laws. The point seems to be that Ridley was, or ought to have been, hanged ; that his carcase, anatomised and stuffed, stood in the Library; and that *"frater scoundrellus"* discovered on his remains the Freemason's Mark. Can this be the

---

* "An Essay on the Earlier Part of the Life of Swift," by Rev. John Barrett, D.D.. and Vice-Provost of Trinity College, Dublin London, 1808. Impressed by Dr. Barrett's arguments, Sir Walter Scott included the Tripos in his edition of Swift's Works, 1814, where it was seen by Dr. Oliver, who failed to realise its historical importance.

earliest hint of the Legend of the Red-hot Poker? The title *Sir* prefixed to some of the names, such as Sir Goodlet and Sir Warren, is the proper Academic style of Bachelors in residence. We have ventured on a translation of the Latin passages. If any reader should deem our version inelegant, we can shelter ourselves behind the hideous dog-Latin of the original.

The speech of the *Terrae Filius* occupies, in the original MS., 35 closely-written quarto pages, and is divided into three Acts or sections, of which the close of the Second and the epilogue to the Third Act alone concern us. We have transcribed the passages from the original MS. in the Library of Trinity College, Dublin, and we now submit them for the information of Masonic students :—

"A TRIPOS or SPEECH,

DELIVERED AT A

COMMENCEMENT in the UNIVERSITY

OF

DUBLIN,

HELD THERE JULY 11, 1688,

BY

JOHN JONES,

THEN A.B., AFTERWARDS D.D.

ACT [Section] I.
[*Nihil ad rem.*]

ACT [Section] II.

" . . . .

It was lately ordered that for the honour and dignity of the University there should be introduced a Society of Freemasons, consisting of gentlemen, mechanics, porters, parsons, ragmen, hucksters, divines, tinkers, knights, thatchers, coblers, poets, justices, drawers, beggars, aldermen, paviours, sculls, freshmen, bachelors, scavingers, masters, sowgelders, doctors, ditchers, pimps, lords, butchers, and tailors, who shall bind themselves by an oath never to discover their mighty no-secret; and to relieve whatsoever strolling distressed brethren they meet with, after the example of the Fraternity of Freemasons in and about Trinity College, by whom a collection was lately made for, and the purse of charity well stuffed for, a reduced Brother, who received their charity as follows :

" From Sawny Richardson, a bottle of ale and two rolls.

" From Mr. Hassett, a pair of old shoes.

" From a kind-hearted butcher at Lazy Hill, a calf's countenance.

" From the Right Honourable Lord Charlemont, a cast hat.

" From long Lawrence, an inch of tobacco.

" From Mr. Ryder, a groat.

" From Dr. Gwithers, an old glister-pipe.

" From Mr. Marsh and Sir Tenison, a bundle of godly ballads.

" From Mr. Smith, an old pair of quilted stockings.

" From a tapster at the sign of the Hog in Armour, a comfit.

" From Sir Goodlet, a piece of an old Smiglesius for a natural use, cunningly procured by the means of Sir Goodlet.

" From Sir Warren, for being Freemasonized the new way, five shillings.

" From Mr. Edward Hall, a pair of cast night gloves.

" Lastly, from Mr. Hancock, a slice of Cheshire cheese; which the hungry brother eat up with such gusto, and liked so well, that he stole away the rest in his breeches.

" Tam libera potitus contributione, frater scoundrellus sarcinulas suas discessurus colligit, et vultu hilariore solito.   Quadrangulum transit ; dumque præ nimio gaudio, porrectiore incedit fronte, altioresque tendit gressus, quisnam inter homines obviam dedit illi, nisi frater fraterrimus Cooper; qui ut fidelem novit hominem, festinatus accurrit, humaniter corripit dextram, utque moris est spississimo conspuit basio: deinde Bibliothecam versus, comiter ambulant ut inter caetera admirabilia Ridlaeum visitent: quem dum hospes curiosis lynceis oculis perscrutatur, et diligentius rimatur, quantum homuncionis judices, carnifex, et medici, reliquerunt, pooh dolor, inter partes, an nobiliores an posteriores nescio, privatum Fraternitatis notavit signum (Anglicè, the Freemasons' Mark).   Quo viso, Dii boni, quanto clamore totam infecit domum.   Ter et saepius pulsavit pectus, exsangues dilaniavit genas, et eheu nimium dilaceratas dilaceravit vestes.   Tandem vero paulo modestius insaniens, hujusmodi versiculis ridiculum effudit dolerem.

[Our Brother, the scoundrel, having become master of so generous a collection, gets his wallets together with a view of making off, and crosses the Square with a more cheerful countenance than usual. And while, through his excess of joy, he advances with head erect and stalks with prancing paces, who of all men came to meet him but the most brotherly of brothers, Cooper! As soon as he recognises this faithful fellow, he runs to him with all speed, cordially grasps his hand, and, as their wont is, beslobbers him with a most glutinous kiss. Thereafter they walk towards the Library, with the object of viewing Ridley among the other wonders of the place. While the visitor is examining him with the prying eyes of a lynx. and is ransacking, with particular care, whatever the judges, the executioner, and the surgeons have left of the poor fellow's carcase, alas! and alas! he descried— whether on the nobler or the hinder parts, I know not for certain—the *Signum* (in plain English, the Freemasons' Mark). As soon as he saw this, good Heavens! with what a yell he filled the building. Over and over again he thumped his breast, lacerated his pallid cheeks, and tore to rags his garments, already, alas! too ragged. After a while, when his paroxysm had cooled down a bit, he poured forth his ludicrous grief in verses after this fashion.]

"EULOGIUM RIDLAEANUM:

"An Elegy upon Ridlev.

" Unhappy Brother, what can be
   In wretchedness compared to thee,
   Thou grief and shame of our Society !

Had we in due time understood
That thou wert of the Brotherhood,
By fraud or force thou had'st got loose
From shameful tree and dismal noose :
And now perhaps with life been blest
As comely a brother as the best,
Not thus exposed a monumental jest ;
When lady longs for college beer,
Or little dame or country squire
Walk out an afternoon, to look
On thee, and devil-raising book ;
Who kindly rather chose to die,
Than blemish our Fraternity,
The first of us e'er hang'd for modesty.
And now, alack, and well-a-day,
Thy parchment hide is stuff'd with hay :
Nay, worse ; the Æsculapians,
Thy mighty misery to enhance,
Have cruelly cut thee out of countenance ;
And, to show witty spite, at once
Preserved thy skin and lost thy bones.
Thus here, in wooden hatch you stand,
With scornful musket at your hand :
The mice' and rats' mock centinel,
A poor ridiculous spectacle
To gibing Joan, to Kate and Nan,
Thou worse than skeleton of man.
So does he measure out his grief,
For loss of Brother and of thief.
Nor less concern'd does Cooper stand ;
But sobbing with his clout in hand,
And destitute of consolation,
Kept time with all his tribulation.
Their grumbling woe runs thro' and thro' them ;
If all were known, 'twould quite undo them.
The sighs which up and downward go,
Their unfeigned sorrow show :
For the devil's in't, if they pretend,
Who vent their grief at either end.

B

" Hoc munere elaborato, non diutius lacrymis indulgent, sed dolore police [pollice?] suppresso, taciti discedunt. Protinus lodgum convocant, fratresque omnes certiores faciunt quantum sibi infamiae, et quantum miseriae infelicissimo accedit fraterculo; graviter luget fraterculus et Societas, et suspiriis ex imo pectore petitis, statim provisum est in posterum, neminem qui crucem meretur, vel qui suspendendus est, in Societatem Freemasonorum admitti; quo authoritate statuto et albo [libro] lodgi prolato, singuli, tam generosi quam scoundrelli, solidissimis basiis promiscuè dicunt valedictionem.

[Having carefully attended to this duty, they give way to tears no longer, but, wiping their eyes on their knuckles [*lit.*, their grief being stifled with the thumb], make off in silence. They summon a Lodge forthwith, and inform all the brethren of the load of disgrace in store for themselves, and of suffering for their most unhappy little brother. The Fraternity and the aforesaid little brother take it greatly to heart, and, amid sighs heaved from the inmost breast, arrangements are made on the spot, that hereafter no one deserving of the extreme penalty of the law, or sure to be hanged, shall be admitted into the Society of Freemasons. As soon as this has been formally ruled, and the Register of the Lodge produced, each of them, gentlemen and scoundrels alike, bids farewell to the other with most solid kisses indiscriminately bestowed.]

END OF ACT [Section] II.

ACT [Section] III.

[In the epilogue, the orator makes rueful reference to the likely results of his afternoon's work, enumerating the various classes whose hostility he has excited.]

"   .   .   I have left myself no friend.   .   .   . If I betake myself to the Library, Ridley's ghost will haunt me, for scandalising him with the name of Freemason.   .   .   The Freemasons will banish me their Lodge, and bar me the happiness of kissing Long Lawrence.   .   .   .   I take my leave.

" FINIS."

The foregoing remarkable quotations demonstrate that the Fraternity of Freemasons was so well known in Dublin in 1688, that a popular orator could count on his audience catching up allusions to the prominent characteristics of the Craft. The speaker was addressing a mixed assemblage of University men and well-to-do citizens, interspersed with ladies and men of fashion, who had come together to witness the chief University function of the year. His use of the theme proves that the Freemasonry known to him and his audience was conspicuous for its secrecy and for its benevolence. We can fairly deduce, too, that membership of the Craft was not confined to Operatives, or to any one class. Otherwise, the catalogue of incongruous callings would be without point.

The importance of such public notice of Freemasonry in 1688 can hardly be overrated. The instances of what may be called public mention of our Brotherhood before 1700 can be counted on the fingers of one hand. They are practically confined to the entries in Elias Ashmole's "Diary," 1646 and 1682; Dr. Robert Plot's diatribe in the "History of Staffordshire," 1686; Randle Holme's observations in "The Academie of Armory," 1688; and Aubrey's memorandum of the preparations for Sir Christopher Wren's Acception in 1691. Even the bare occurrence of the word Freemason before 1700 is thought to be of such moment, that antiquaries hunt it down with the ardour of hounds pursuing game. The evidence that the upper classes of Society in Ireland were well acquainted with Freemasonry and its tenets before William of Orange landed there, will come somewhat as a surprise. But the proof is beyond cavil. The testimony, coming from an unsympathetic outsider, is akin in its nature to that of Dr. Robert Plot, and quite comparable to it in historical value.

The story of the Tripos and its circumstances is much more interesting than the rigmarole itself, which, indeed,

B I

would hardly deserve even passing attention but for its bearing on the history of Freemasonry. Some day, perhaps, the opportunity may arise for telling again that long-forgotten tale.

It is impossible to credit Swift with any share in the composition. But it is equally impossible that he should have been unacquainted with Freemasonry and its doings. The real author and he were intimate, and the conditions of college life render it incredible that one should know and the other should not know the Society on which the main illustration of the Tripos depended. Swift must have been acquainted with Freemasonry, if it were only through having been present at the Tripos.

Seven-and-thirty years have to elapse before we find again such public mention of the Craft, that we can positively affirm Swift must have had cognisance of it. Not many months before Swift started for London in 1726, the Fraternity of Freemasons in Ireland had conducted a public ceremony on such a scale that all Dublin rang with the noise of the celebration. On St. John's Day, 1725, the Earl of Rosse, Grand Master, attended by his Grand Wardens, was escorted by a brilliant and numerous company of Brethren through the streets of Dublin. The procession must have challenged Dean Swift's notice, for it started from Werburgh-street, within a stone's throw of the Deanery. When Swift resumed his stated course of life in Dublin, after the terrible dislocation by growing mental disease that followed on the death of Stella, he found the Fraternity again astir with Lord Kingston's reorganisation of the Irish Grand Lodge in 1729-30. We have thus two periods in which the claims of the Craft forced themselves specially on his attention. The first formed a prologue, the second an epilogue to the visits to London, during which he was the guest of one and the intimate associate of another Freemason. Both periods bore testimony to the increasing popularity of the Craft by the publication of pamphlets, in which its secrets were attacked or defended.

The representative publication of the former period was "The Grand Mystery of Freemasons Discover'd," of which the first edition was published in 1724, and the second in 1725. Only half-a-dozen copies of these editions are known to exist in the public and private libraries of Europe, and two or three more have found their way to the United States. The first edition has been brought within the reach of students by the careful facsimile executed under the direction and at the expense of that munificent bibliophile, Bro. E. T. Carson, of Cincinnatti, U.S.A. A similar service has been rendered to the second edition by our own Bro. Robert Freke Gould, who has appended a reprint of it to his invaluable "History of Freemasonry." This pamphlet is the archetype of the innumerable Spurious Rituals that have since appeared. It purports to give the secrets of Freemasonry in the form of a catechism, embroidered with words ostensibly of Hebrew origin. It prefixes certain linear figures, which it calls Freemasons' signs, and concludes with other methods or "signs" by which "to know a true Mason." The former set of signs, styled "Guttural," "Pedestal," "Manual," and "Pectoral," is simply unintelligible; and the latter set is ludicrous beyond belief.*

By way of retort to the "Grand Mystery," there appeared in Dublin a broadsheet entitled *The Free-Mason's Vindication, being an Answer to a scandalous Libel intituled* THE GRAND MYSTERY of THE FREE-MASONS DISCOVR'D, &c. *Wherein is plainly prov'd the Falsity of that Discovery, and how great an Imposition it is on the Publick.* This broadsheet, under date 1726, is preserved in the British Museum, and was reprinted, with a somewhat erroneous comment, in the *Freemasons' Magazine and Masonic Mirror,* 1859, and more carefully in *The Kneph,* 1886.

---

* Dr. Oliver, in his entertaining romance, "The Revelations of a Square," makes an heroic attempt to explain the linear signs. His explanation can be read backwards or forwards with equal appropriateness.

Its literary merits are no whit above those of the
"Grand Mystery." The only sign of intelligence it
betrays is in personally applying to the author of the
"Grand Mystery" the fable of the Sour Grapes, as a
counterpoise to a droll story applied by him to depreciate the value of the secrets of Freemasonry.

Of a very different order from the "Vindication" is
the pamphlet to which we have more than once alluded
when discussing Swift's connection with the Craft,
entitled "A Letter from the Grand Mistress of the Free-
Masons, to George Faulkner, Printer." This pamphlet
has been rescued by Bro. Henry Sadler from the oblivion
into which treatises, called forth by a passing occasion,
so readily fall, and from which not even the name of
Swift could preserve this ephemeral production. When
the occasion passes, the interest of the ordinary reader
ceases. A century or two must then elapse before the
interest of the antiquarian reader awakens.

In common with other minor pieces by Swift, the
"Letter from the Grand Mistress" leaves something to
be desired by the bibliographer. We can do no more
than approximate to the date of its composition, or of
its first publication. These two dates do not necessarily
coincide in the case of Swift's minor writings. He
frequently kept pieces by him for years before sending
them to press, if, indeed, he ever sent them at all.
When they did see the light in type, they were as often
as not pseudonymous or anonymous. No author ever
cared less to claim the paternity of his compositions :
he did not even trouble himself to make pecuniary profit
from them. The only book by which he made money
was "Gulliver's Travels," and that was owing to Pope's
bargaining on his behalf. When a father is so careless
of his family, outsiders find it hard to calculate the exact
ages of the children. It would help us if we knew whether
the tract was originally published as a separate pamphlet,
or as a Letter to some one of the score of Journals
that lived, and, for the most part, died in Dublin between
1725 and 1735.

As the " Letter from the Grand Mistress " is addressed to George Faulkner, it might be supposed that it was addressed to him in his capacity of editor of *Faulkner's Dublin Journal,* of which the first number was published 27th March, 1725. But this does not seem so clear from the promise the author makes on page 379 : " Next week shall be published," etc. For in those days *Faulkner's* was not a weekly journal. The *Dublin Weekly Journal* was the property of a rival bookseller, known as Jemmy Carson, almost as odd a character in his way as Faulkner. The " Letter " does not appear in any copy of these newspapers preserved in Dublin, but the early series are so incomplete as to admit of no certainty. In fact, it may be taken that as a painstaking search through the public libraries has failed to light on the " Letter " in its original form, no absolute conclusion can be reached as to the date or the mode of its publication.

George Faulkner (1699-1775), to whom the " Letter " was addressed, and to whom we are indebted for the preservation of many of Swift's minor works, was the first Irish printer to earn a name for himself. How well executed some of his work was may be judged from the facsimile of the " Letter," which is reproduced from the edition of Swift's works, published by him in Dublin, 1760–9. He was almost as well known on one side of the Channel as the other, so that Foote found it worth while to impersonate him on the London stage under the name of Peter Paragraph, a sort of ancestor of the dreaded Interviewer of to-day. He was in London at the time of Swift's last visit, and, if the Register of 1730 were complete, we should expect to find his name in it. For he is stated to have been an active Freemason in his early days, though his zeal could not stand against political pressure in his old age.

Faulkner did not become the Dean's printer, in succession to the luckless Harding, till 1726. A year or two must have elapsed before he attained importance enough for the " Letter " to be addressed to him as a prominent citizen. Hence we may assume that the

"Letter" was not published till 1727, or even later, though it was written in parody of a Spurious Ritual earlier by some years. Whatever its date, internal evidence shows it had reference to the "Grand Mystery," and not to Prichard's "Masonry Dissected." The allusions to "Guttural," "Pectoral," and other signs and words, which we need not particularise, leave little room for doubt on the point. The assonance between "The Grand Mystery" and "The Grand Mistress" may well have suggested the central idea of the book.

The version of the "Freemason's Song" appended is consistent with the same date. It fails to include the verse we have shown elsewhere to have been written by Springett Penn, Deputy G.M. of the Grand Lodge of Munster. It is probably the best known of all the verses :—

> We're true and sincere,
> And just to the fair ;
> They'll trust us on ev'ry occasion.
> No mortal can more
> The Ladies adore
> Than a Free and an Accepted Mason.

Springett Penn composed this verse for his Grand Lodge, which was absorbed by the Grand Lodge of Dublin about 1730. It had got into such general acceptance by 1734 that Bro. William Smith inserted it in the English edition of his "Pocket Companion," printed in 1734, and Dr. Anderson himself annexed it bodily in 1738. So we can deduce that this "Letter from the Grand Mistress" was published before the new verse reached Dublin—that is, before 1730.

The other piece of verse prefixed to the title of "The Grand Mistress" does not help us much in determining the date. It belongs rather to the evidence of authorship. It would go far to settle that question, if it should ever come to be doubted that Swift was the writer. For the simile of Ixion and the cloud was used by Swift both before and after "The Grand Mistress." It is to be found in the opening paragraph of the "Tritical Essay on the Faculties of the Mind" written, probably, as early as the year 1712. In this Essay Swift simulates to the life the sham learning and barren platitudes in which the moralists almost outdid the eighteenth-century panegyrists of Freemasonry. In 1733, Swift recast the passage to suit his " Answer " to Dr. Sheridan's " New Simile for the Ladies." The later form of the passage runs as follows :—

> To disappoint Ixion's rape,
> Jove dress'd a cloud in Juno's shape :
> Which, when he had enjoy'd, he swore
> No goddess could have pleased him more;
> No difference could he find between
> His cloud and Jove's imperial queen;
> His cloud produced a race of Centaurs,
> Famed for a thousand bold adventures.

The method in which Swift rehandled the idea leaves no doubt that he was the author of both forms. The reference to an imaginary source, " A.B.C., lib. 6, p. 107," is quite in Swift's line. A similar alphabetical signature is appended to his " Letter to the Dublin Weekly Journal," 25th Oct., 1729. This " Letter " affords a further parallel to " The Grand Mistress." It contains an impersonal allusion to the Drapier, just as the Postcript to " The Grand Mistress " refers to " your ingenious Drapier, to whose pen we, as well as the rest of the nation, own ourselves obliged." This mention of the Drapier shows that his identity was still under a veil. The passage must, therefore, have been written before 7th November, 1729, when Swift publicly acknowledged the authorship of the " Drapier's Letters," of which the last had been published five years before.

All we know of Swift's habits and mental condition goes to corroborate the likelihood of 1727-1729 as the date of the composition, if not of the publication, of " The Grand Mistress." We must remember, however, that it is still within the domain of uncertainty, and may be overset by a single fortunate discovery.

In default of such a discovery of the Dublin original, the earliest edition of Swift's collected works to which we can trace " The Grand Mistress " is the London

edition of his "Miscellanies" (crown 8vo., 1745-8).
The first volume, published in the year of the Dean's
death, was followed by twelve others, with varying
dates on the title pages. The eleventh volume, containing "The Grand Mistress," has the date 1746. The
trade custom of issuing the volumes of Swift's Works in
irregular sequence, to meet the demand for a particular
work, makes the bibliographer's task difficult. In the
present set, Vol. XI. bears date 1746, while Vols. VIII.
and IX. are of 1748. George Faulkner was a great
offender in this way. He printed off Swift's works in
large quantities, kept the sheets in stock, and issued
the separate volumes from time to time with new title
pages. All we need say of his editions is, that he over-
persuaded the Dean, sorely against his will, to let him
bring out a selection in four volumes 1735. This was
the first attempt of the kind in Dublin, and was rein-
forced by volume after volume of additional matter,
amidst which we find "The Grand Mistress" in due
course. Finally, George Faulkner admitted "The Grand
Mistress" to a permanent place in what he intended to
be his masterpiece—his great definitive edition of
Swift's Complete Works, 1760-9, extending eventually to
twenty volumes 8vo. The reproduction is from Vol. X.
of this edition, and the title-page of the particular volume
bears date 1762.

This Dublin edition of 1760-9 remained the standard
until Sir Walter Scott's edition in nineteen volumes,
1814. Sir Walter, who was himself a Freemason, thought
fit to silently omit "The Grand Mistress." Since then
it has dropped out of Swift's Works. Dr. Kloss, in
his *Bibliographie der Freemaurerei*, while noting its
appearance in a German version in the edition of
Swift's Works, published at Hamburg and Leipzig in
1760, observes that it is absent from the more recent
editions.

From the time that Swift became anxious about
Stella's health till his mind gave way in 1736, he sought
distraction in the composition of trifles in prose and

verse, in mock English, in dog Latin, in every style that could while away the saddened hours. Some of these are on topics, compared with which Female Freemasonry appears respectable and important. But all bear the mark of his peculiar humour. His literary method is utterly unlike those of the other great humourists. It effects great ends, but it runs great risks. All men can understand the broad guffaw of Rabelais, the kindly smile of Cervantes, or the lipless sneer of Voltaire. But many men stand agape before Swift's impenetrable mask. Over and over again critics, whom it would not be fair to describe as dullards, have been beguiled by his superhuman command of countenance into treating his extravagant paradoxes as serious arguments.* The effect of his solemn irony was greatly heightened by his singular power of suiting his style to the occasion. Even in his familiar letters, acute critics have noted three distinct styles, into each of which Swift dropped without effort, so as to suit his correspondent.

The " Letter from the Grand Mistress," though a very indifferent production, shows the characteristics of Swift's method, and is no worse than a score of other trifles thrown off by his fevered brain. He pursues his usual plan. He selects a theme of extreme absurdity, and he proceeds to treat it as a matter of course. In the " Letter," Female Freemasonry poses as the crucial absurdity, just as in another pamphlet of this period, " The Modest Proposal for preventing the Children of poor People in Ireland from being a Burden to their Parents or Country," the conversion of the children into articles of food stands as the kernel of absurdity. Each theme is treated in a style artfully adapted to the matter in hand. The " Modest Proposal" treats its subject in the formal language and with the self-satisfied air of an agricultural M.P. debating the importation of colonial

---

* Swift's imperturbable solemnity froze even Dr. Oliver's fluency. The Doctor, who mentions " The Grand Mistress " in " The Revelations of a Square," did not know what to make of it. He dismisses it in two lines of text and an extract in a footnote.

foodstuffs. "The Grand Mistress" seizes the salient points of the Spurious Ritual, and adds to the counter-feit learning and the blundering grammar of "The Grand Mystery" a feminine inconsequence of her own.*

To the word of warning rendered necessary by the general character of Swift's method, another may be added, inspired by the particular character of the treatise under consideration. The "Letter from The Grand Mistress" is not a skit upon Freemasonry. It is a caricature of a pretended exposure of Freemasonry. The more grotesque features of the exposure are reproduced; they could hardly be exaggerated. The "Grand Mystery" professes to reveal the secrets of the Craft "as they were found in the custody of a Free-mason who dyed suddenly"—a figment that was to serve the turn of many a subsequent impostor. The "Grand Mistress" out-Herods this with the story of a country lodge befogged by the fumes of the punch bowl. The veneer of Rabbinical learning is outdone by grotesquely twisting the Hebrew alphabet. The absurdity of the signs could not well be heightened, but their nonsense is made clear: and so on to the end of the tale.

There is room for suspicion that the Bees of Egypt and France, and the other make-believe pedantries, so ostentatious in their irrelevance, point obliquely at Dr. Anderson's imaginative "History." Swift was ever a hater of shams.

The location of the peccant lodge at O-m-gh (pre-sumably Omagh, the county town of Tyrone) affords no real clue. Non-Regular, or St. John's Lodges, may have

---

* Swift deals with the concoctors of the Spurious Rituals much in the same way as he had dealt with the Deists in the "Argument to prove that the Abolition of Christianity in England may, as things now stand, be attended with some Inconveniences, and perhaps not produce those many good Effects proposed thereby;" or with the pseudo-metaphysicians in the "Tritical Essay on the Faculties of the Mind." in suiting his style to the pinchbeck original, Swift hit on the very style of Peter Paragraph himself. "The Letter from the Grand Mistress" is so exactly in the manner of George Faulkner when he turned biographer of the Dean, that, if it had come a score of years later, it might well be credited to him.

existed in Ulster in Swift's time, as we know they did in Munster. The probability is greatly increased, it must be acknowledged, by the testimony we have adduced as to the existence of such Lodges in Leinster in 1688 , and that, too, within Dean Swift's knowledge. Freemasonry certainly took strong hold of the county in the latter half of the eighteenth century, for there are 92 lodges on the Register of 1800. But the earliest lodge we can trace in the county dates from 6th September, 1759, when a warrant was issued for Omagh to Pat. Hamilton, Esq., James MtGomery, John Hall, and nine others. This lodge continued at work till 1843, when it became dormant, but was revived in 1848. It is worth noticing that the warrant was granted to Patrick Hamilton, Esq., a namesake, and, we believe, a relative of that Capt. Hamilton, of Castle Hamilton, who was a fellow guest with Swift in 1728 at Gosford, in the contiguous county of Armagh. After the shock of Stella's death in 1728, Swift was induced by Sir Arthur and Lady Acheson to pay them a visit at Gosford. This visit lasted the better part of a year, and, if we were to judge by inferential evidence, would be a most likely time for him to have written " The Grand Mistress." To distract his mind from his grief, he threw off a great number of fugitive pieces, of which this treatise might well form one.

The paragraph that associates the Knights of St. John of Jerusalem and of Malta with "the famous old Scottish lodge of Kilwinnin," will not fail to strike the student conversant with the development of chivalric Degrees. The passage reads much more as if it were written after 1760 than before 1730. The early mention of the Druids and the Rosicrucians is equally suggestive. Doctor McGregor, " now Professor of Mathematicks at Cambridge," is a myth : at least, no such graduate can be found in the University Register.

It will be observed that we have treated only of the outward form, and not of the real matter of "The Letter." The reason is obvious. As Dean Swift himself puts it, quoting the great Lord Somers, "Wise men neither admit nor deny what fools attribute to them." If Freemasons were to deny this or that absurdity, they would be held to admit the rest.

The Spurious Rituals are without authority. Hence they are of little weight as records of the rites practised by Freemasons ; but they are of the highest interest as records of what contemporary outsiders thought those rites to be. "The Grand Mystery" was designed for those who did not know, not for those who did know, the secrets of Freemasonry. It shows what the outsiders of 1724 expected. With that, its historical importance ends.

"The Grand Mistress" is equally important. But its importance is of a different kind. It is not a satire on Freemasonry, but a travesty of a pretended exposure of Freemasonry. It has no exact counterpart in the literature of the Craft. The only parallel we remember to have seen is the curious tract entitled "Free Masons examin'd; or, the World brought out of Darkness into Light," published by Alexander Slade, of Norwich, in 1754. This is, in a sense, a parody of the Spurious Rituals. But Slade was innocent of satire. His aim was to elevate—an aim that entails failure, unless directed by genius.

If the "Letter from the Grand Mistress" had any claim to be taken as a genuine disclosure of the secrets of Freemasonry, discussion of its subject-matter would be, in the highest degree, inexpedient. As it is only a solemn-faced travesty of a pretended exposure, such discussion would be ludicrous.

W. J. CHETWODE CRAWLEY.

A LETTER

FROM

THE GRAND MISTRESS

OF THE

FEMALE FREEMASONS.

A LETTER from the GRAND MIS-
TRESS of the FREE-MASONS, to
GEORGE FAULKNER, Printer.

Ixion *impious, lewd, profane,*
Bright Juno *woo'd, but woo'd in vain.*
Long had he languish'd for the Dame,
'Till Jove, *at length, to quench his Flame;*
Some say for Fear, some say for Pity,
Sent him a Cloud like Juno *pretty,*
As like as if 'twere drawn by Painters,
On which he got a Race of Centaurs,
A Bite quoth VENUS.—
                    A. B. C. Lib. 6. Pag. 107.

A LETTER, &c.

SEEING it is of late become a Fashion in
Town, in Writing to all the World, to
addrefs to YOU, our Society of *Female Free
Mafons*

Mafons hath alfo chofen you for our *Printer;* and fo, without Preface, Art, or Embellifh-ment, (for Truth and a fhort Paper needeth none of them) our *Female Lodge* has the whole Myftery as well as any *Lodge* in *Europe,* with proper Inftructions in Writing; and what will feem more ftrange to you, without the leaft Taint of *Perjury.* By this Time any *Reader* who is a *Mafon,* will, I know, laugh, and not without Indignation : But that matters not much, our Sex hath long owed yours this good Turn: You refufed to admit Queen *Elizabeth,* and even *Semiramis,* Queen of *Babylon,* altho' each of them (without *Punning*) had a great deal of *Male Flefh* upon their Bodies ; but at laft you will be forced to own we have it; and thus it was we came by it.

A GENTLEMAN who is a great Friend to all our Members, who hath fince inftructed and formed us into a *Lodge,* and who we therefore call our *Guardian,* fell in lately with a *Lodge* of *Free Mafons* at *O--m--gh* in *Ulfter.* They preffed him hard to come into their Society, and at length prevailed. They wanted an *Old Teftament* to fwear him by. The *Inn-keeper's* Bible having both *Old* and *New* bound up toge-ther, would not do: For the *Free Mafon's* Oath being of a much older Date than the *New Teftament,* that is from the Building of *Solo-mon's* Temple, (for until then it was but a Pro-teftation well larded over with *Curfes* and *Exe-crations*)

crations) they are always ſworn on the *Old Teſtament* only. They offer to buy the Fellow's *Bible*, he conſents ; but finding they were to cut away the *New Teſtament* from the *Old*, concluded them, at once, a Pack of profane Wretches, and very piouſly reſcued his *Bible.* This Cuſtom of ſwearing on the *Old Teſtament* only, is what hath given Birth to the vulgar Error, that *Free Maſons* renounce the *New Teſtament.* So they proceed on to the reſt of the Ceremony, deferring the Oath until next Morning, one of them having an *Old Teſtament* for the Purpoſe at his Houſe hard by. This, it is true, was a heinous Blunder againſt the Canons of *Free Maſonry.* But the Gentlemen were far gone in *Punch* and *Whiſky.* In ſhort, our Friend and preſent Guardian is made a *Free* and *Unſworn Maſon*, and was three Hours gone on his Journey next Morning, before the merry *Free Maſons* awoke to ſend for their *Old Teſtament* ; and what was worſe, they had taught him the Form of the Oath, againſt he was to ſwear in the Morning.

Now, as to the ſecret Words and Signals uſed among *Free Maſons*, it is to be obſerved, that in the *Hebrew* Alphabet, (as our Guardian hath informed our *Lodge* in Writing) there are four Pair of Letters, of which each Pair is ſo like that at firſt View, they ſeem to be the ſame, *Beth* and *Caph, Gimel* and *Nun, Cheth*

and

and *Thau*, *Daleth* and *Refch*, and on thefe depend all their Signals and Grips.

CHETH and *Thau* are fhaped like two ftanding Gallowfes of two Legs each ; when two *Mafons* accoft each other, the one cries *Cheth* and the other anfwers *Thau*, fignifying that they would fooner be hanged on the Gallows, than divulge the *Secret*.

THEN again *Beth* and *Caph* are each like a Gallows lying on one of the Side-Pofts, and when ufed as above, imply this pious Prayer : *May all who reveal the* Secret, *hang upon the Gallows 'till it falls down.* This is their *Mafter Secret*, generally called the *Great Word*.

DALETH and *Refch* are like two Half Gallowfes, or a Gallows cut in two, at the crofs Stick on Top, by which when pronounced, they intimate to each other, that they would rather be half-hanged, than name either *Word* or *Signal*, before any but a *Brother*, fo as to be underftood.

WHEN one fays *Gimel*, the other anfwers Nun; then the firft again joining both Letters together, repeats three times together *Gimel-Nun, Gimel-Nun, Gimel-Nun*, by which they mean that they are united as one in Interefts, Secrefy, and Affection. This laft Word hath, in Time, been depraved in the Pronunciation from *Gimel-Nun* to *Gimelun*, and at last into *Giblun*, which Word being by fome Accident difcovered they, now a-days, pretend is but a *Mock-Word*.

ANOTHER

ANOTHER of their Words hath been maimed in the Pronunciation by the Illiterate, that is the Letter *Lamech*, which was the *Huſh Word*, for when ſpoke by any *Brother* in a *Lodge*, it was a Warning to the reſt to have a Care of Liſteners. It is now corruptly pronounced *Lan*, but the *Maſons* pretend this alſo is a *Mock Word*, for the ſame Reaſon as *Giblin :* This Play with the *Hebrew* Alphabet, is very antiently called the MANABOLETH.

WHEN one *Brother* orders another to walk four Steps backwards ; four, becauſe of the four Pair of Letters already mentioned, and backwards becauſe the *Hebrew* is writ and read backwards.

As to their *Myſterious Grips* they are as follow : If they be in Company, where they cannot with Safety ſpeak the above Words, they take each other by the Hand, one draweth one of the Letters of the *Manaboleth*, with his Finger on the other's Hand, which he returneth as in ſpeaking.

IT is worth obſerving, that a certain *Lodge* in Town, publiſhed ſometime ago, a Sheet full of *Mock Maſonry*, purely to puzzle and banter the Town, with ſeveral falſe Signs and Words, as *Mada* or *Adam*, writ backwards, *Boas, Nimrod, Jakins, Pectoral, Guttural*, &c. but not one Word of the real ones, as you ſee by what hath been ſaid of the MANABOLETH.

AFTER King *James* the Sixth's Acceffion to the Throne of *England,* he revived Masonry, of which he was *Grand-Mafter.* Both in *Scotland* and *England,* it had been entirely fuppreffed by Queen *Elizabeth,* becaufe fhe could not get into the Secret. All Persons of Quality, after the Example of the King, got themfelves admitted *Free-Mafons;* but they made a Kind of MANABOLETH in *Englifh,* in Imitation of the true and antient One; as I. O. U. H. a Gold Key, that is, *I owe you each a Gold Key;* H. CCCC his Ruin. *Each forefees his Ruin.* I. C. U. B. YY. for me. *I fee you be too wife for me.* And a great Deal more of the fame foolifh Stuff, which took its Rife from a filly *Pun* upon the Word *Bee;* for you muft know, that ———

——— A *Bee* hath in all Ages and Nations, been the Grand *Hieroglyphick* of *Mafonry,* becaufe it excels all other living Creatures in the Contrivance and Commodioufnefs of its *Habitation* or *Combe;* as among many other Authors, Doctor *Mc. Gregor,* now Profeffor of Mathematicks in *Cambridge* (as our Guardian informeth us) hath learnedly demonftrated; nay, *Mafonry* or Building, feemeth to be of the very Effence or Nature of the *Bee,* for her building not the ordinary Way of all other living Creatures, is the generative Caufe which produceth the young ones, (you know, I fuppofe, that *Bees* are of *neither Sex.)*

FOR

For this Reaſon the Kings of *France*, both *Pagans* and *Chriſtians*, always eminent *Free-Maſons*, carried three *Bees* for their *Arms*, but to avoid the Imputation of the *Egyptian* Idolatry of worſhipping a *Bee*, *Clodovæus* their firſt Chriſtian King, called them *Lilies*, or *Flower-de-Luces*, in which, notwithſtanding the ſmall Change made for Diſguiſe Sake, there is ſtill the exact Figure of a *Bee*. You have perhaps read of a great Number of Golden Bees found in the Coffin of a *Pagan* King of *France*, near *Bruſſels*, many Ages after CHRIST, which he had ordered ſhould be buryed with him, in Token of his having been a *Maſon*.

The *Egyptians*, always excellent and antient *Free-Maſons*, paid Divine Worſhip to a *Bee* under the outward Shape of a *Bull*, the better to conceal the Myſtery, which *Bull* by them called *Apis*, is the *Latin* Word for a *Bee*; the *Ænigma* of repreſenting the *Bee* by a *Bull* conſiſteth in this; that according to the Doctrine of the *Pythagorean Lodge* of *Free-Maſons*, the Souls of all the *Cow-kind* tranſmigrate into *Bees*, as one *Virgil* a Poet, much in Favour with the Emperor *Auguſtus*, because of his profound Skill in *Maſonry*, hath deſcribed; and Mr. *Dryden* has thus *ſhow'd*.

———————————————— *Arieus*
Four Altars raiſes, from his Herd he culls
For Slaughter, Four the faireſt of his *Bulls*,

B b 2   Four

Four Heifers from his Female Store he took,
All fair, and all unknowing of the Yoke;
Nine Mornings thence with *Sacrifice* and
                    [*Prayers,*
The Gods invok'd, he to the Groves repairs:
Behold a Prodigy ! for from within
The broken Bowels and the bloated Skin;
A buzzing Noile of *Bees* his Ears alarms,
Straight iffue thro' the Sides affembling
                    [Swarms, *&c.*

WHAT *Modern Mafons* call a *Lodge* was for
the above Reafons, by Antiquity call'd a HIVE
of *Free Mafons.* And, for the fame Reafons,
when a Diffention happens in a *Lodge,* the going off and forming another *Lodge,* is to this
Day called SWARMING.

OUR Guardian is of Opinion, that the prefent *Mafonry* is fo tarnifhed by the Ignorance of
the Working, and fome other illiterate *Mafons,*
that very many, even whole *Lodges,* fall under the Cenfure of the venerable *Chinefe Brach-
man,* whofe Hiftory of the Rife, Progrefs, and
Decay of *Free-Mafonry,* writ in the *Chinefe*
Tongue, is lately tranflated into a certain *Euro-
pean* Language. This *Chinefe* Sage, fays, the
greateft Part of current *Mafons,* judge of the
Myfteries and Ufes of that facred Art, juft as a
Man perfectly illiterate, judgeth of an excellent Book, in which, when opened to him, he
findeth no other Beauties than the regular U-
niformity in every Page, the Exactnefs of the
                                        Lines

Lines in Length, and Equidiſtance, and Black-
neſs of the *Ink,* and Whiteneſs of the *Paper,*
or as the famous *Britiſh Free-Maſon* MERLIN
ſayeth of the Stars in the Firmament, when
viewed by a *Child,* &c.   But I ſhall not trouble you with the Length of the Quotation at
preſent, becauſe *Merlin* and Fryar *Bacon,* on
Free-Maſonry are ſoon to be dreſſed up in modern *Engliſh,* and ſold by our Printer, Mr.
Faulkner, if duly encouraged by Subſcribers;
and alſo a Key to *Raymundus Lullius,* without
whoſe Help, our Guardian ſays, it is impoſſi-
ble to come at the Quinteſſence of *Free-Maſonry,*

BUT, ſome will perhaps object, how came
your unſworn Guardian by this refined and uncommon Knowledge in the great Art? To
which I anſwer, That,

THE Branch of the *Lodge* of *Solomon's* Temple, afterwards called the *Lodge* of St. *John* of
Jeruſalem, on which our Guardian fortunately
hit, is, as I can eaſily prove, the antienteſt and
pureſt now on Earth.   The famous old *Scot-
iſh Lodge* of *Killwinin,* of which all the
Kings in *Scotland* have been, from Time to
Time, Grand Masſters without Interruption,
down from the days of *Fergus,* who reigned
there more than 1000 Years ago, long before
the Knights of St. *John* of *Jeruſalem,* or the
Knights of *Malta,* to which two *Lodges* I muſt
neverthelefs, allow the Honour, of having

B b 3   adorned

adorned the antient *Jewish* and *Pagan Mafon-ry*, with many Religious and Chriftian Rules.

Fergus being eldeft Son to the chief King of *Ireland*, was carefully inftructed in all the Arts and Sciences, efpecially in the natural Magick, and the Cabaliftical Philofophy (afterwards called the *Roficrufians* by the *Pagan Druids* of *Ireland* and *Mona*, the only true *Cabalifts* then extant in the *Weftern* World for they had it immediately from the *Phœnicians, Chaldeans,* and *Egyptians*, which (tho' but a Woman I can prove,) the *Egyptians* probably had it immediately from *Abraham*, as the Scripture plainly hinteth in the Life of that Patriarch ; and, it is allowed, I am told by Men of Learning, that the *Occult* as well as *Moral* Philofophy of all the *Pagans* was well befprinkled and enriched from the Cabaliftical School of the Patriarchs, and afterwards by the *Talmudifts* and other inferior *Rabbins*, altho' the prevailing Idolatry of thofe Days much depraved and vitiated it.

Fergus, before his Defcent upon the *Picts* in *Scotland*, raifed that famous Structure called to this Day *Carrick-Fergus* after his Name, the moft myfterious Piece of Architecture now on Earth, (not excepting the Pyramids of the *E-gyptian* Mafons, and their *Hieroglyphicks* or *Free-Mafons* Signs) as any fkilful *Free-Mafon* may eafily perceive by examining it according to the Rules of the Art ; he built it as a *Lodge* for his College of *Free-Mafons*, in thofe Days called

called *Druids*, which Word, our Guardian aſ-
fureth us, ſignifieth an *Oak* in the *Greek* Language, becauſe *Oak* is one of the beſt Timber-
Trees for Building, of which, (eſpecially the
Marine Architecture,) the *Druids* were the
only Maſters, although your Modern Term
of *Maſon* implieth no more than a Worker in
Stone, erroneouſly enough indeed, or at leaſt
far ſhort of the true and antient Term of
Druid, ſince the Marine Architecture, the
moſt uſeful Branch of that ſacred Art, corre-
ſpondeth naturally and perfectly with the Word
Druid, or *Worker* in *Oak*, and had nothing at
all to do with Stones of any Kind, until *Jaſon*,
a famous *Druid*, or *Free-Maſon*, uſed the *Loadſtone* when he went in Queſt of the *Golden-
Fleece*, as it is called in the enigmatical Terms
of *Free-Maſonry*, or more properly ſpeaking
of the *Cabala*, as Maſonry was called in thoſe
Days. The Uſe of the *Loadſtone* was then,
and long after, kept as ſecret as any of the
other Myſteries of the Art, until by the una-
nimous Conſent of all the Great *Lodges*, the
Uſe of it was made publick for the common
Benefit of Mankind. *Jaſon's* artificial *Frog*
had it fixed in his Mouth, and having a free
Swing in an oaken Bowl, half filled with Water, always faced the *North* Pole, which gave
Riſe to the poetical Fable ; that *Jaſon's* Frog
was a *Little Familiar*, or *Sea Demon* preſiding
over the Navigation like any other Guardian

Angel ;

Angel; for, *Free-Masons* in all Ages, as well as now, have been looked upon to deal with *Sprites* or *Demons*, and hence came that Imputation which they have in many Nations lain under, of being *Conjurors or Magicians* ; witnefs *Merlin* and Friar *Bacon*.

IT is perhaps further worth remarking, that *Jason* took one of the two Sacred Vocal Oaks of the Grove of *Dodona*, to make the Keel of the *Argus*, for fo his Ship was called, myfterioufly joining together *Architecture* or *Mafonry*, and the *Druidical* Priefthood or Power of explaining the Oracles. For, our Guardian will have it fo, that the *Pagan* Priefthood was always in the *Druids* or *Mafons*, and that there was a perceivable Glimmering of the *Jewifh Rites* in it, although much corrupted, as I faid ; that the *Pagan* Worfhip was chiefly in Groves of *Oak*, that they always looked upon the *Oak*, as facred to *Jupiter*, which Notion is countenanced (making Allowance for the *Paganifm)* by the *Patriarchs* ; for you fee in *Genefis*, that *Abraham* facrificed under the Oaks of *Mamre*. *Jofhua* indeed took a great Stone and put it up under the *Oak*, emblematically joining the two great Elements of *Mafonry* to raife an Altar for the LORD.

OUR Guardian alfo fays that *Cæfar's* Defcription of the *Druids* of *Gaul* is as exact a Picture of a *Lodge* of *Free-Mafons* as can poffibly be drawn.

HIS

HIS Reaſons for *Manaboleth* are the better worth diſcovering, that I believe there are even ſome *Maſons* who know nothing of it, *viz.* that it hath been an antient Practice among the *Cabaliſtick Philoſophers* to make every *Hebrew* Letter an *Hieroglyphick*, myſterious in its Figure above all other Letters, as being thus ſhaped and formed by the immediate Directions of the *Almighty*, whereas all other LETTERS are of *Human Invention*.

SECONDLY, that the *Manaboleth* hath a very cloſe and unconſtrained Analogy with *Maſonry* or *Architecture*, for that every Letter of the *Hebrew* Alphabet, as alſo of the *Syriac*, *Chaldaic*, and *Iriſh* Alphabets, derived from it, have their Names from *Timber-Trees*, except ſome few which have their Names from *Stones:* And, I think, it is pretty plain, that *Timber* and *Stone* are as much the Elements of *Maſonry* as the Alphabet is of *Books*, which is a near Relation enough between *Architecture* and *Learning* of all Kinds, and naturally ſheweth why the *Druids*, who alſo took their Title from a Tree, kept *Learning* and *Architecture* jointly within themſelves.

NEXT Week ſhall be publiſhed the *Free-Maſon's* Oath, with the Remarks upon it of a young *Clergyman* who hath petitioned to be admitted *Chaplain* to our *Lodge*, which is to be kept at Mr. *Prater's* Female Coffee-Houſe every *Tueſday* from Nine in the Morning to
Twelve,

Twelve, and the Tenth Day of every Month in the Year; where all Ladies of true Hearts and found Morals fhall be admitted without Swearing.

I THINK it proper to infert the *Free-Mafon's* SONG commonly fung at their Meetings, altho' by the by, it is of as little Signification as the reft of their Secrets. It was writ by one *Anderfon*, as our Guardian informeth me, juft to put a good Glofs on the Myftery, as you may fee by the Words.

S O N G.

I.

COME let us prepare
We Brothers that are
Affembled on merry Occafion,
Let's drink, laugh, and fing,
Our Wine has a Spring;
Here's a Health to an Accepted MASON.

II.

The World is in Pain
Our Secrets to gain,
And ftill let them wonder and gaze on,
They ne'er can divine
The Word or the Sign,
Of a Free and an Accepted MASON.

III.

'Tis this and 'tis that,
They cannot tell what,

Why

Why ſo many great Men of the Nation,
    Shou'd Aprons put on,
    To make themſelves one,
With a Free and an Accepted MASON.

IV.

    Great Kings, Dukes and Lords,
    Have laid by their Swords,
Our Myſtery to put a good Grace on ;
    And ne'er been aſham'd,
    To hear themſelves nam'd,
With a Free and an Accepted MASON.

V.

    Antiquity's Pride
    We have on our Side,
And it maketh Men juſt in their Station ;
    There's nought but what's good,
    To be underſtood
By a Free and an Accepted MASON.

VI.

    Then join Hand in Hand,
    To each other firm ſtand,
Let's be merry and put a bright Face on :
    What Mortal can boaſt
    So noble a Toaſt,
As a Free and an Accepted MASON.

POST-

POSTSCRIPT.

Mr. *Faulkner,*

OUR *Lodge* unanimoufly defire you will give their fincere Refpects to your *Ingenious* DRAPIER, to whofe *Pen,* we, as well as the reft of the Nation, own ourfelves obliged.   If he be not already a *Free-Mafon,* he fhall be welcome to be our *Deputy Guardian.*

Your Humble Servant,

THALESTRIS.

Tfrif eht Tfugua Nilbud*.

* DUBLIN, *Auguft the* firft.   *Thofe who* underftand Irifh, *may find fome other Meaning.*

EXPLANATORY INTRODUCTION

TO

"A DEFENCE OF FREE-MASONRY, &c."

D

EXPLANATORY INTRODUCTION

TO

"A DEFENCE OF FREE-MASONRY, &c."

AS this volume will probably fall into the hands of some who may not be familiar with the minor details of the history of English Freemasonry, I have deemed it advisable, in order that they may the better understand and appreciate the value of these Reprints to give a clear account of the Masonic conditions under which they were originally published. Bro. Chetwode Crawley shared this opinion with me, and, in treating of the first of our Reprints, has produced evidence to show that the Freemasonry of England and Ireland was, and, indeed, could not well help being, the same until "variations" were admittedly introduced in the English working. It now becomes my duty to take up the story subsequent to these "variations," and to give a brief sketch of the two Grand Lodges mentioned in the second pamphlet we reproduce.

For about sixty years prior to the year 1813 there were two Grand Lodges in London, and in the year last named they were both active and prosperous, each having many subordinate lodges under its jurisdiction in nearly every part of the civilized world. The older of these bodies was established in the year 1717, and has been variously designated " The Grand Lodge of Free and Accepted Masons of England," " The Regular Grand Lodge," " The Modern Grand Lodge," and later, " The Grand Lodge under the Prince of Wales," George Prince of Wales, afterwards King George the Fourth, having been its Grand Master from 1790 to 1813.

The other Grand Lodge started in the year 1751 as a Grand Committee which blossomed into a Grand Lodge two years later. This body was known as " The Grand

D I

Lodge of the Antients," or, to give it its full description, "The Grand Lodge of Free and Accepted Masons according to the Old Institutions." Its members were also designated " Athole Masons," because two Dukes of that name had presided over them as Grand Masters. For the sake of brevity and as a simple distinction these two Societies were, and still are, referred to by Masonic writers as Antients and Moderns, the Antients being the organization of 1751, and the Moderns that of 1717.

At first sight this description of them naturally appears somewhat strange, but it can be explained in this way.

The regular Grand Lodge of 1717, although un-doubtedly the elder as an organized body, had, for certain reasons which were thought good at the time, so varied the ceremonies and deviated from the old customs of the Craft, that, according to their opponents of 1751, they had forfeited their right to the title of Antient, while they themselves, having preserved the traditional usages and ceremonies unaltered, were the real Antient Masons, and no doubt there was a certain amount of truth in these allegations. As may be readily imagined, a strong and bitter rivalry existed between the two Societies for many years, promoted and fostered I regret to say chiefly by the leading Masons on both sides. In fact it was at first a struggle for absolute power and supremacy on the part of the Moderns—the older and possibly more respectable community—and for existence as an organization on the part of the Antients, who were stigmatised by their rivals as seceders, schismatics, rebels, while even still more offensive terms were applied to them, on the principle, I suppose, of any stick being good enough to beat a dog with.

For want of knowledge of the true circumstances, those epithets have been persistently applied to the Antients by Masonic writers all over the world from about 1775 until 1887, when I took upon myself the task of trying to prove, with my pen, that the opprobrium which had been so freely showered upon them had no justification whatever; that on this particular subject Masonic historians were in error. I said then, and I say now, that there is not a particle of evidence in existence to prove, or even indicate, that a single member of the lodges that formed their Grand Committee in 1751 had ever owned allegiance to the Grand Lodge of 1717; that all the available evidence bearing on the subject is strongly opposed to the theory of secession, and if these Brethren had not seceded from the older body they could not have been either schismatics or rebels, and we had no right to apply those epithets to them.

I said also that they had a better right to the title of Antients than those who had modernized the ceremonies and departed from the old customs; that the term Antient had no reference whatever to their age as a consolidated or governing body, but only to their customs and their mode of working, for they called themselves Antients before they combined to form a Grand Lodge.

My opinions and evidence were published in 1887 in a small book, entitled "Masonic Facts and Fictions," wherein I asserted that the greatest fiction in Freemasonry was the accepted version of the origin of the Antient Grand Lodge. As may be supposed the advent of this book created no small sensation amongst the recognised historians of the Craft, and it naturally met with considerable opposition. It is, however, most gratifying to me to be able to announce that most of my former opponents have acknowledged their acquiescence in the new and somewhat startling theory then propounded. This result speaks volumes for their candour, for it was due rather to the strength of the case than to any art or eloquence on the part of the advocate.

I will state, in as few words as possible, the substance of that theory. It is that the brethren who formed the Antient Grand Lodge were not English Masons at all, but chiefly Irish Masons, with Irish customs and cere-monies, or old English customs and ceremonies, for, no doubt, the working was identical, or nearly so, in both countries before the English Grand Lodge sanctioned innovations.

I will readily admit that there may have been old English and Scotch Masons amongst them, but the great majority of them were undoubtedly Irish to the backbone.

The researches which Bro. Dr. Chetwode Crawley has been pursuing for years in Ireland, and which he has published in "Cæmentaria Hibernica" and elsewhere, have thrown a flood of light on our early Freemasonry. I am proud to say that every fresh discovery he has made has been confirmatory of my theory, and what is most striking is that his researches have generally been directed to points where my evidence was weakest, with the result that he has been enabled to fill up several gaps in my argument.

In the course of years the anger of these two rival Societies became softened ; they found that neither of them could gain the mastery, and as they became better acquainted they learned to respect each other, and, naturally so, for they were both animated by the same noble motive—the dissemination of the grand principles of Brotherly Love, Relief, and Truth.

After several attempts in that direction, in the year 1809 active steps were taken by the Moderns to bring about an union with those they had at first treated with contempt and then with angry abuse and misrepresentation. It was not, however, until their Grand Lodge had passed the following resolution that the Antients would listen to their overtures : " That this Grand Lodge do agree in opinion with the Committee of Charity, that it is not necessary any longer to continue in force those measures which were resorted to in, or about, the year 1739, respecting irregular Masons, and do therefore enjoin the lodges to revert to the ancient land-marks of the Society."*   Here we have two important admissions,

---

* Grand Lodge Minutes, April 12, 1809.

first that they had departed from the ancient land-marks, and secondly, they were not certain when that departure had taken place.

Owing to the exertions of some of the more enlightened members of both Grand Lodges, an Union, on terms mutually honourable, was finally consummated in the year 1813, and this important event was ratified and confirmed with great rejoicing and much pomp and ceremony in the Grand Hall of the English Fraternity in London. Since this period our Society has been known as the United Grand Lodge of Antient, Free, and Accepted Masons of England.

Probably the rarest, and, to my thinking, the most important, from an historical point of view, of the additions made to the Grand Lodge Library in recent years, is the pamphlet here reproduced, for the original of which we are deeply indebted to the W. Bro. William James Hughan, Past Grand Deacon of England.

Notwithstanding that the Author's modesty, or some other reason, prevented the publication of his name, this little book is of great value, not alone on account of its rarity, but because it contains information which seems to have escaped the notice of all our historians, from Preston downwards. Bro. Hughan casually mentions the pamphlet as being in the unrivalled Masonic Library of Bro. Carson, of Cincinnati, and quotes it in his " Origin of the English Rite of Freemasonry"; but even he was not familiar with the whole of its contents, until this copy came into his possession. It will be seen that it tends to confirm my pet theory of the Irish origin of the Antient Grand Lodge. As Bro. Hughan did not accept that theory, it was most gratifying that he, with characteristic frankness and generosity, having pointed out the several passages tending to confirm my views, at once asked my acceptance of the valuable *brochure*, though many Masonic Collectors would gladly have paid handsomely for its possession. However, finding that there is not a copy of the book in the British Museum, nor in England, so far as I know, I considered that its proper home would be in the Grand Lodge Library, where it would be accessible to all who might be able to avail themselves of the opportunity thus afforded for perusing its pages, intending ultimately to reproduce it for the benefit of the ever-extending and rapidly-increasing band of students of the history of our Order, and also that, in the event of the original being lost or destroyed, we should not be without a *facsimile* of it.

I have no intention of entering upon a strict examination of this pamphlet; it will, no doubt, suffice for present purposes if I point out a few paragraphs which seem to bear on the early organization of the Antients.

To begin with the Title-page. The words "Under the Constitution of the English Grand Master" would seem to imply that some other Grand Master, not English, was in the writer's mind when arranging this portion of his work, although, as a matter of fact, the "English Grand Master" at that period was an Irishman—Lord Blayney.

Of the contents of the pamphlet itself little need be said, abuse of the Antients forms its distinguishing feature; but it will be observed that the nameless writer never once intimates that these people *seceded from the regular Grand Lodge*. He does, however, say that they are "chiefly Natives of Ireland," and therein consists the real value of the book. His disparaging remarks as to their social and intellectual status must be taken for what they are worth, as coming from a partizan of the rival body who in all probability had little actual knowledge of the people he was abusing.

Fortunately their first register of members is still available, and from it we learn that many of them belonged to the artizan class, and that is about the worst that can, with justice, be said of them. I should ill discharge my editorial functions if I failed to point out certain discrepancies between the statements of the anonymous author and recorded facts as set forth in the minutes of the proceedings of the Antient Grand Lodge.

On page 18 he says, in effect, that the Grand Master of Ireland "refused to countenance them." The following appears in the minutes of the 1st of March, 1758:—"Heard a Letter from Mr. John Calder (G.S.) in Dublin wherein he assured the Grand Lodge of Antient Masons in London that the Grand Lodge of Ireland did mutually concur in a strict union with the Antient Grand Lodge in London and promised to keep a Constant Correspondence with them."

"Order'd that the Grand Secretary shall draw up an Answer in the most Respectful and Brotherly Terms wherein the General thanks of this Grand Lodge shall be convey'd, and assure them that we will to the utmost of our powers promote the welfare of the Craft in General."

Ibid, 2nd June, 1762. "Heard a Letter from Grand Secretary Calder in Ireland in answer to a former letter written by Secretary Dermott to the Grand Lodge of Ireland, proposing a Continual Correspondence, &c."

"Order'd that a Constant Correspondence shall be kept with the Grand Lodge of Ireland.

"And whereas the Grand Lodge of Ireland have agreed and firmly Resolved not to admit any Sojourner from England (as a Member or Petitioner, &c.) without producing a Certificate (of his good behaviour) under the seal of the Ancient Grand Lodge in London. It is hereby Order'd and Declared, That from and after the first day of July in the year of our Lord One thousand seven hundred sixty and Two all and every Sojourner or Sojourners from Ireland shall produce proper Certificates or other necessary Recommendations from the G. Sec. of Ireland before he or they can be admitted as a Member or receive any part of the General Charity."

In answer to the statement on page 18, "that a certain *noble* Peer permits them occasionally to use his name though he never presides in any of their Assemblies," I can only say that the Earl of Blesinton, who as Viscount Mountjoy had been Grand Master of Ireland in 1738-39 was elected Grand Master of the

Antients 1st Dec., 1756, and by his own consent was re-elected every year until 1760, when he was succeeded by the Earl of Kelly from 1760 to 1765, and that both these noblemen performed the usual functions of their office by signing Warrants, &c.

The time that has elapsed since the publication of the pamphlet renders it extremely difficult to identify the author of it. Masonic writers at that period were of the *rara avis* species. As, however, an expression of opinion will probably be expected from me, I may say at once that I am disposed to ascribe the authorship either to the Grand Secretary then in office, Samuel Spencer, or to his predecessor, John Revis, Grand Secretary 1734-56, and Deputy Grand Master 1757-63, the last-named being the more likely. These officials must have been cognizant of the real origin of the Antient Grand Lodge, and in substance and tone the pamphlet bears a striking resemblance to a letter written by Spencer's successor in 1769 (printed at length in " Masonic Facts and Fictions "). wherein the writer mentions "the late Mr. Revis" as his authority for an assertion relative to the Antients, which, like many other stories from the same quarter, has no foundation in fact.

It is not easy to account for the scarcity of the pamphlet under notice, for no doubt a large number were distributed. The most probable explanation that occurs to me is that being an official, or inspired, publication it was suppressed shortly after its appearance, or when, some years later, it was decided by the Modern authorities to issue a new version of the origin of the Antients—that of secession from the Grand Lodge of England. To the best of my knowledge this fable first appeared in Preston's "History of Masonry," published in the Grand Lodge Calendar in 1775-76. The story is cleverly told and very plausible, but it differs materially from this pamphlet, for there is not a word in it to indicate the Irish origin of the Antients, nor is Ireland even mentioned. I was not aware of the existence of " A Defence of Free-Masonry, &c.," when defending Laurence Dermott and his associates in 1888-89 from the attack then made upon them. The letters reprinted, however, in a subsequent portion of this volume will show that while so engaged I was unwittingly dealing with aspersions of a similar character which had been cast upon these brethren more than a hundred and twenty years previously.

HENRY SADLER.

A
DEFENCE
OF
FREE-MASONRY,

As practised in the
REGULAR LODGES,

Both FOREIGN and DOMESTIC,

Under the *Constitution* of the

ENGLISH **GRAND-MASTER.**

In which is contained,

A REFUTATION of Mr. *Dermott*'s abfurd and ridiculous Account of FREE-MASONRY, in his Book, entitled AHIMAN REZON; and the feveral *Queries* therein, reflecting on the *Regular* MASONS, briefly confidered, and anfwered.

What fhall be given unto thee ? or what fhall be done unto thee, thou falfe Tongue ? PSALM 120, *v.* 3.

To the above Defence is added,
A Collection of Mafons ODES and SONGS, moft of them entirely new, and never before printed.

LONDON:
Printed for the AUTHOR, and fold by W. FLEXNEY, near *Gray's-Inn Gate, Holborn*; and E. HOOD, near *Stationers-Hall, Ludgate-Street.* 1765.

[Price One Shilling.]

A
DEFENCE
OF
FREE-MASONRY.

THE Reaſon for the following *Pamphlet* appearing in Print, proceeds entirely from the *hearty good Wiſhes and Love* I bear to the *Right Worſhipful Fraternity* of FREE and ACCEPTED MASONS, and not from any lucrative or ſiniſter Motives; the Truth of which, I hope will appear to the Satisfaction of every Brother, who will take an impartial View of what is here offered in Defence of the REGULAR LODGES.

A Book, entitled AHIMAN REZON (a new Edition of which was printed laſt Year) very lately fell into my Hands, and the Peruſal of it (though an old MASON, who

had

had neglected the *Lodges* feveral Years) rouzed my juft Refentment, and I determined to take up my *Pen* (though in no Refpect equal to the Tafk) in Defence of this Ancient and Honourable Brotherhood, which is moft fcandaloufly *traduced*, by the malevolent *Author* of that *Book*.

My Intention is not to fcrutinize into every Part of his *new-coined Conftitution-Book*, efpecially the ridiculous Story of the fh-tt-n End of * *Daniel Tadpole*, the *Author* of *The three diftinct Knocks*, and one of his *Ancient Brethren*.

As a *Mafon*, I do not wifh Mr. *Dermott* fo wretched and untimely an End as poor *Tadpole*, notwithftanding he may think him juftly rewarded for his Publication; but when *he* dies (were I to have the ordering of his *Funeral*) he fhould be buried thus.

Previous

* He fays that *Tadpole* being purfued by *Bailiffs*, efcaped into *Whitechapel-Fields*, and hid himfelf in a Sand, or Clay Pit, where he flept till Night, when a *Nightman* came with a Cart full of Human Ordure, and emptied it upon him, which fmothered him to Death.

Previous to the Interment, a capacious *Pit* fhould be dug, in an extenfive *Valley* (or in the *Valley* of *Jehofophat*, if in his Life-time he fhould prefer that Place to any other) and I would have his *Corpfe* preceded by *Ancient Mafons*, of the following Profeffions or Callings, *viz. Scavengers* and *Nightmen*, who fhould bear upon their Poles the *Enfigns* of his *Order*, *viz.* the *Crofs Pens*, pendant, in green, red, or yellow *Ribbands*, or any other * *tawdry* Colour he is now moft fond of, and a dirty Leather Apron, lined and bordered with the fame Colour, on which may be wrote, in as legible Characters as poffible, Ahiman Rezon. The *Deacons* Rods to be carried by two *Chimney-Sweepers*, and the *Columns* by a walking Poulterer, who retails Rabbits, &c. in the Streets, and a brawny Chairman, all of the fame Country, and likewife *Ancient Mafons.* Immediately

* The *Grand Lodge* of *Englifh* Masons, have ordered, for Diftinction fake, that none but the *Grand Officers*, fhall ever wear *Jewels* of *Gold*-pendant to *blue Ribbands.* But Mr. *Dermott*, in Oppofition to that *Law*, afferts, that every Member of the *Grand Lodge* has a Right to wear *blue*, or any other Colour. Happy are the Regular Masons, that they have no fuch refractory Members, to difpute the Authority of the Grand Lodge, and fet up Opinions of their own.

mediately·preceding the *Hearse*, inftead of a Number of pampered *Churchmen*, chanting a *folemn Dirge*, I would have a *dead March*, played by fome Rabble, on *ancient Britifh, and Hibernian Inftruments, viz.* the *Salt-box* and *Rolling-pin, Wooden Spoons, Marrow-bones and ·Cleavers, Hurdy-gurdys, Frying-pans and Iron Skewers, &c. &c. &c.*   Then the *Corpfe,* properly habited as an *Ancient Mafon* (with the laft *Edition* of his *Book* in his Left Hand, and a *Pen* in his Right) borne on an open *Hearfe, i. e.* a *Cart*, on which they ufually carry dead *Horfes*, and fometimes *Affes*, that the Public may have a diftinct View of the Figure of a Man, fo eminent for Scandal, Defamation, *&c.* and to put them in Mind (if he thinks it will be of any real Service to him) to offer up an Ejaculation for the Re-pofe of his *Soul.*   The *Hearfe* to be follow-ed, not by his *Relations*, but by as many *Nightmen* as there were Builders in *Solomon's Temple*, every one with a *Cart* loaded with their ufual *Commodity* ; and after his *Remains* are depofited in the *Pit*, every Man fhould empty his *Cart* upon him ; fo large a Quan-tity being doubtlefs due to his great Merit. There will be no occafion for *Caffia, Spikenard, Myrrh,* or any other Perfumes ufed in em-

balming

balming the Dead, as that will yield a fufficient Odour, and will not only fave Time,
Labour and Expence, in building a Monu-
ment of Stone, but will alfo tranfmit his
Memory to Pofterity, more than AHIMAN
REZON can be expected, or even a *Maufo-
leum* as large as that built for the *King* of
Caria, which was ufually reckoned the
fourth Wonder of the World. After the
Funeral is over, his *Friends* (if he has any)
may furround the *Valley*, fing *Mafs*, and fet
up a *Howl*, according to the Cuftom of their
Country.

But to return to my Subject; I fhall only
fpeak of fuch Parts of his *wonderful* Publication, which he has compiled for the Ufe of
Ancient Mafons; at the Beginning of which,
" *be folemnly declares, before God and Man,*
" *that he has not the leaft Antipathy againft*
" *the Gentlemen Members of the modern Society*
" *of Mafons,*" as he is pleafed to call them
(Thanks to him for the Appellation.) How
far this be true, let the candid Reader
judge.

This *Genius* (if I may fo call him) begins
his Remarks on the *Hiftory* of MASONRY,
which

which was compiled from the ancient Records, and Manufcripts of FREE-MASONS, of *Italy*, *Scotland*, and many in the Hands of private Brethren, in different Parts of *England*; and becaufe he is, beyond Doubt, incapable of writing an *Hiftory* of it himfelf, he attacks *that* which hath received the Approbation of both the *Great* and the *Learned*, and (under the Similitude of a Dream)* with an Effrontery peculiar to his *Country*, ridicules both the *Hiftory*, and the *Compilers* of it, fome of whom were as great Men, perhaps, as ever employed their Pens on that, or any other Subject.

Though MASONRY may be, and is with great Propriety traced from the Creation, yet the FREE-MASONS Faculty, and ancient univerfal Practice of converfing without
fpeaking,

* He tells us, that when he had fat down, with Intention to write an *Hiftory* of *Mafonry*, he fell into a Slumber, and dreamt that SHALLUM, AKKUB, TALMON and AHIMON, who were the four principal *Porters* in *Solomon*'s Temple, appeared to him, and told him, that all Accounts of the Temple were imperfect, except thofe of the Prophets *Jeremiah*, *Ezekiel* and *Ezra*, and alfo *Jofephus*. That even all *their* Works put together would not be fufficient for a Preface to the *Hiftory* of *Mafonry*, and that all other Writers thereof knew nothing of the Matter.

fpeaking, and of knowing each other by *Signs* and *Tokens* (which, fays an old Tradition, they fettled upon the *Difperfion,* or *Migration)* certainly took its Rife from the Confufion of Dialects at the Building of *Babel*; and this Tradition was always firmly believed by the MASONS, the Affertions of this *vifionary* Writer to the contrary notwithftanding : Befides, it is recorded of *Nimrod* * or *Belus,* that he was the firft who reduced Men into Society and Union, which is an additional Argument in favour of the faid Tradition. It is likewife very evident, that FREE-MASONRY has always gone Hand in Hand with the Arts and Sciences, particularly with *Geometry* and *Architecture,* and wherever *they* flourifhed moft, *there* the CRAFT received the moft Encouragement, as well as the greateft Improvement.

That FREE-MASONRY took its Name at the building of *Solomon's Temple,* I believe none but our *dreaming* Author will affert, as fome Traditions affirm, that the Word *Free* was added, becaufe the *Mafons* taught their

B   *Art*

---

* Belus fignifies Lord, and Nimrod was a Name given him by the *Ifraelites,* by way of Invective.

Art to the *Free-born* only, which was their conſtant Practice more than nine Centuries before that Period.

It is however certain that both FREE and OPERATIVE MASONRY, received the greateſt Improvements under King *Solomon*, *Hiram* King of *Tyre*, *Hiram Abbif*, the greateſt *Cabaliſts*, as well as the greateſt *Architects*, then in the World; and ſince then, there haſ been ſcarcely a Building of any Conſequence carried on, in any Country, but ſuch of the Workmen concerned therein, as were FREE-MASONS, conſtantly held a Lodge in, or near it.

An old Record relates, that " *Euclid* the
" famous *Geometer* of *Tyre*, came to the
" Court of *Ptolomy Soter*, and was by him
" encouraged to teach *Geometry*, particularly
" to the Children of the great *Lords* of the
" Realm, who by continual Wars, and De-
" cay of the Sciences in former Reigns,
" were reduced to great Neceſſities to get
" a competent and honourable Livelihood.
" And having received Commiſſion, he
" taught ſuch as were committed to his
" Charge, the Science of *Geometry*, and to
" work

" work in Stone, all Manner of Buildings,
" such as *Temples, Altars, Towers, &c.* and
" gave them Charge to this Purpose, *viz.*
" To be true to their *King*, and to the
" Lord they served, as well as to the *Fel-*
" *lowship* whereof they were admitted ; To
" be true, and love one another, and call
" each other *Fellow* or *Brother.*

" That they should appoint the Wifeft of
" them to be *Mafter* of the Work ; that the
" *Lord* fhould be well ferved, and *they* not
" afhamed ; and many other Charges he
" gave them, too long to be inferted, to
" which he made them fwear a great *Oath,*
" which they ufed at that Time. Thus
" was the CRAFT grounded there ; and
" *Euclid* gave it the Name of *Geometry,*
" which is now called MASONRY."

Hence it appears that FREE-MASONRY
is derived from operative MASONRY, and
therefore wherever the Hiftory mentions the
Building of any great Edifice, we have generally fome Account of the Progrefs and
Succefs of FREE-MASONRY, which fuffici-
ently fhews the Utility, as well as Neceffity
of connecting the Hiftory of one with the

B 2 Progrefs

Progreſs of the other, notwithſtanding Mr. *Dermott*'s Query, *Whether ſuch Hiſtories are of any real Uſe to the Craft ?*

I ſhall ſay no more in Defence of the Utility and Authenticity of the *Hiſtory* of MASONRY, but ſhall only add the Approbation which is ſubjoined to the firſt *Book* of CONSTITUTI‑ ONS ever printed in this (or any other) King‑ dom, in vulgar Year of MASONRY 5723.

APPROBATION.

WHEREAS by the Confuſions occaſioned in the *Saxon, Daniſh,* and *Norman* Wars, the Records of *Maſons* have been much viti‑ ated, the FREE-MASONS of *England* twice thought it neceſſary to correct their *Conſtitu‑ tions, Charges,* and *Rugulations* ; firſt in the Reign of King *Athelſtan* the *Saxon,* and long after in the Reign of King *Edward* IV. the *Norman :* And whereas the old *Conſtitutions* in *England,* have been much interpolated, mangled, and miſerably corrupted, not only with *falſe* Spelling, but even with many *falſe* Facts, and groſs Errors in Hiſtory and Chro‑ nology, through Length of Time, and the Ignorance of Tranſcribers, in the dark and illeterate Ages, before the Rivival of *Geo‑ metry*

metry and ancient *Architecture,* to the great
Offence of all learned and judicious Brethren,
whereby alfo the Ignorant have been de-
ceived.

And our late worthy GRAND-MASTER,
his Grace the *Duke* of *Montague,* having ordered the Author to perufe, correct, and di-
geft, into a new and better Method, the
Hiftory, Charges, and *Regulations* of the ancient *Fraternity* ; he has accordingly examined
feveral Copies from *Italy* and *Scotland,* and
fundry Parts of *England,* and from thence
(though in many things erroneous) and from
feveral other ancient *Records* of *Mafons,* he
has drawn forth the above written new *Conftitutions,* with the *Charges,* and general *Regulations.* And the Author having fubmitted
the whole to the Perufal and Corrections of
the late and prefent *Deputy Grand-Mafters,*
and of other learned Brethren , and alfo of
the *Mafters* and *Wardens* of particular *Lodges,*
at their *Quarterly Communication* : He did
regularly deliver them to the late GRAND-
MASTER himfelf, the faid Duke of *Montague,* for his Examination, Correction and
Approbation ; and his *Grace,* by the Advice
of feveral *Brethren,* ordered the fame to be
handfomely

handſomely printed for the Uſe of the *Lodges*, though they were not quite ready for the Preſs during his *Maſterſhip.*

Therefore *We*, the preſent GRAND-MASTER of the *Right Worſhipful* and *moſt ancient Fraternity* of FREE and ACCEPTED MASONS, the *Deputy Grand-Maſter*, the *Grand-Wardens*, the *Maſters* and *Wardens* of particular *Lodges* (with the Conſent of the *Brethren* and *Fellows*, in and about the Cities of *London* and *Weſtminſter*) having alſo peruſed this Performance, do join our laudable *Predeceſſors* in our ſolemn *Approbation* thereof, as what we believe will fully anſwer the End propoſed; all the valuable *Things* of the old *Records* being retained, the Errors in *Hiſtory* and *Chronology* correǎed, the *falſe* Facǎs, and the *improper* Words omitted, and the Whole digeſted in a *new* and *better* Method.

And we ordain that Theſe be received in every particular *Lodge*, under our Cognizance, as the only *Conſtitutions* of FREE and ACCEPTED MASONS amongſt us, to be read at the making of new *Brethren*, or
when

when the *Maſter* ſhall think fit ; and which the new *Brethren* ſhould peruſe before they are *made.*

Sign'd,

PHIPIP DUKE OF WHARTON,
GRAND-MASTER.

J. T. DESAGULIERS, L. L. D. and F. R. S.
DEPUTY *Grand-Maſter.*

JOSHUA TIMSON, } *Grand-Wardens.*
WILLIAM HAWKINS, }

And the *Maſters* and *Wardens* of 20 *Lodges.*

Since which Time the *Conſtitution-Book* has been twice corrected and reprinted, firſt by Dr. *Anderſon,* in the *Earl* of *Darnley's Grand-Maſterſhip* ; and laſtly by the Reverend Mr. *Entick,* in the *Grand-Maſterſhip* of the *Marquis* of *Carnarvan,* both which times it was inſpected by a *Committee* of *worthy* and *learned* Brethren.

Mr. *Dermott* in the next Place attempts to prove the *Authenticity* of (what he ſtiles) *Ancient Maſonry,* and would feign inſinuate that FREE-MASONRY, as practiſed in the Lodges under the *Engliſh Conſtitution* (of which

which there are near 340) is of modern Invention. He tells us, by Way of Question and Answer, that *Ancient Masonry* is universal, and that *Modern Masonry* is not so.

To which I answer, that our List of *Lodges* is sufficient to prove the contrary, as *that* contains, by far, a greater Number, regularly constituted by the *English* GRAND-MASTER, than there are by any other GRAND-MASTER whatever; together with a great many *Lodges* in different foreign Parts, which are also constituted and governed by *Provincial Grand-Masters*, under our Constitution, which is certainly an evident Proof of the Universality of *English Masonry*.

He then asserts, that an *Ancient Mason* can discover his very Thoughts to a Brother, in the Presence of a *Modern*, without *his* being able to distinguish that either of them are MASONS.

This may pass for Truth with a *Novice* in the Art, or with an entire *Stranger* to it, but an intelligent MASON will laugh at such an idle Assertion. But I suppose he wrote this with a View to draw in the Credulous and Unweary into their *Lodges*.

With

With Regard to the Difference between *Ancient* and *Modern* MASONS, there is certainly a great deal, the former being as remarkable for their *Tautology* and *Prolixity*, as the latter are for their *Brevity*; as the one like a *Methodiſt* Teacher, who attempts to preach extempore, will engroſs the whole Evening, in ſpinning out a *tedious* Lecture, while the other, like an *orthodox* Divine, delivers the Subſtance of the ſame Lecture (which fully anſwers the Purpoſe, and renders it much more agreeable) in leſs than an Hour. And I believe every ſenſible MASON will allow this to be the moſt material Difference, notwithſtanding Mr. *Dermott*'s Aſſertion to the contrary.

He then tells us that a *Modern* MASON may with Safety communicate all his *Secrets* to an *Antient*, but an *Ancient* cannot do ſo to a *Modern*, without further *Ceremonies.*

It is true, an *Engliſh* MASON may ſafely communicate all his Secrets to either *Scotch* or *Iriſh* MASONS, provided they have been made in Lodges *regularly* conſtituted by their reſpective GRAND-MASTERS, and ſo, *viſe verſa*; for as MASONRY is univerſal, there

C

is

is nothing in it, which one *regular* MASON ought to conceal from another; but the *English* MASONS should be cautious with whom *they* converse, as there are many *irregular* MASONS, *i. e.* made in *Lodges* under the Title of *Ancient*, or *York*, who some time ago pretended to be *constituted* or *authorized* by the GRAND-MASTER of *Ireland*, who (by the bye) I am credibly informed, refused to countenance them, as it would be highly absurd for one GRAND-MASTER to constitute *Lodges* in the Territories of *another*. However it is said that a a certain *noble* Peer permits them occasionally to make use of his Name, though he never presides in any of their Assemblies.

The next thing which he affirms is, that the Number of *Ancient Masons*, compared with the *Moderns*, are as ninety to one, which (according to his Assertion) proves the Universality of the *old* Order.

I have already observed, that the Number of *Lodges*, under the *English Constitution*, by far exceeds those of any other, consequently the Number of MASONS must be so in Proportion, which must also set his boasted *Universality* aside.

Again,

Again, he informs us that Sir. *Chriſtopher Wren* having ſerved the Crown fifty Years, was at laſt diſplaced at the Age of ninety, in favour of another, which was the Cauſe of his neglecting the *Lodges*, and as the MASONS refuſed to hold any *Communication* under his *Succeſſor*, they in Time had almoſt forgot their Leſſon, and that (*Maſonry* as now practiſed in the *Ancient Lodges*, was preſerved in the *Lodges* at *York*, without Alteration or Addition ; but) about the Year 1717, being deſirous of reviving the *Order*, they again aſſembled, and being very *ruſty*, they determined to make up the Deficiency with a new *Compoſition*, and to render the Whole more pliable to the Humours of the Times ; in order to which (among other things equally *ſcandalous* and *ridiculous*, he ſays, that) they agreed, that every Perſon during the Time of his *Initiation*, ſhould wear *Boots*, *Spurs*, a *Sword* and *Spectacles*. That they ſhould likewiſe wear their *Aprons* reverſed, *i. e.* the lower Part being faſtened round the *Abdomen*, or *Paunch*, with the *Bib* and *Strings* dangling downwards, to prevent the *Gentlemen* from looking like ſo many *Mechanicks*, and to convince the Spectators, that there was not a *working Maſon* among them.

C 2 It

It has been the conſtant Practice of all *good Maſons* to bridle that unruly Member, the *Tongue*, and never to ſuffer it *to lye againſt a Brother, but rather to let it hang in his Defence*; but this *ungenerous* Brother, contrary to all the Laws of *Maſonry*, is determined, (if poſſible) to bring Diſgrace upon the whole *Fraternity*, and is as profuſe with his *very* little Stock of Wit, as a young Spendthrift *Heir* of a large *Eſtate.*

What he ſays concerning Sir *Chriſtopher Wren*, I beg Leave to contradict, by obſerving, that his Age and Infirmities prevented his Attendance on that extraordinary Occaſion of laying the laſt Stone on the Top of the *Lantern* of St. *Paul's Cathedral*, which obliged him to depute his Son *Chriſtopher Wren*, Eſq; to perform that Office for him, in the Preſence of Mr. *Strong*, and his *Son,* *Grand-Wardens*, as alſo the *Fellow Crafts*, chiefly employed in the building of that Edifice ; by which it appears, that Sir *Chriſtopher* did not neglect the *Craft*, on account of his being diſplaced, but by reaſon of his Infirmities and great Age only : For it is reaſonable to ſuppoſe, that a Man of his Years could not attend *That*, or any other Society, so frequently as when younger. Neither was it ever known, that his Successor Mr. *Benson*, was proposed to succeed him as GRAND-MASTER, nor did the *Masons* continue a great while without one, for the *Cathedral* of St. *Paul* was finished in the Year 1710, and though, through his Disability, he did not attend the Lodges, he was, nevertheless, acknowledged their GRAND-MASTER for some Time after,* till the *Craft* observing that the *Lodges* suffered greatly for want of his Presence, as usual, in visiting and regulating their *Meetings*, they then thought it necessary to cement under a new GRAND-MASTER. For this Purpose (as the *History* of the *Craft* informs us) the *Lodges*,

1. At the *Goose and Gridiron, in St. Paul's Church-yard.*

2. At the *Crown in Parker's-lane, near Drury-lane.*

3. At

* I wonder he has not the Confidence to affirm, that they had almost forgot their Lesson a second time, during the five Years *Grand-Mastership* of a *noble* Lord, about twelve Years since; who, though he seldom attended the *Quarterly Communications*, the Business thereof was conducted by his *Deputy*, and Wardens, and the particular Lodges continued their Meetings as usual.

3. *At the Apple Tree Tavern, in Charles-street, Covent-garden.*

4. *At the Rummer and Grapes Tavern, in Channel-row, Westminster.*

And some *old Brothers* met at the said *Apple Tree*; and having (as usual on such Occasions) put into the Chair the oldest *Master-Mason* (being the Master of a Lodge) they *constituted* themselves a GRAND-LODGE *pro Tempore*, in due Form, and forthwith revived the *Quarterly Communication* of the Officers of *Lodges* (called the GRAND-LODGE) resolved to hold the *Annual* ASSEMBLY and FEAST, and then to chuse a GRAND-MASTER from among themselves, till they should have the Honour of a NOBLE *Brother* at their Head.

Accordingly,

On St. JOHN BAPTIST's Day, in the third Year of King GEORGE I. A. D. 1717, the ASSEMBLY and FEAST of the FREE and ACCEPTED MASONS, was held at the aforesaid *Goose and Gridiron*; now removed to the *Queen's Arms* Tavern in St. *Paul's Church-yard.*

Before

Before Dinner, the *oldeft Mafter Mafon* (being the *Mafter* of a *Lodge*) in the Chair, propofed a Lift of proper Candidates, and the Brethren, by a Majority of Hands, e-lected

Mr. ANTHONY SAYER, *Gentleman*, GRAND-MASTER of MASONS, who being forthwith invefted with the Badges of Office and Power, by the faid *oldeft Mafter*, and inftalled, was duly congratulated, and ho-maged by the Affembly.

Mr. *Jacob Lamball*, Carpenter, } *Grand-*
Capt. *Jofeph Elliot*, } *Wardens.*

And on St. *John's Day*, 1718, GEORGE PAYNE, Efq; was elected GRAND-MASTER, at whofe Requeft feveral old Manufcripts of the GOTHIC *Conftitutions* were produced and collated.

The GRAND FEAST was again held *June* 2 , 1719, when JOHN THEOPHILUS DESAGULIERS, L. L. D. and E. R. S. was proclaimed GRAND-MASTER, who revived feveral *ancient* Ufages. In this *Grand-Mafter-*
fhip

ship, several *Noblemen* were admitted into the *Craft*, and several *new Lodges* were constituted.

At the ensuing FEAST, *June* 24, 1720, GEORGE PAYNE, Esq; was again proclaimed GRAND-MASTER. This Year several very valuable *Manuscripts* were produced (for they had nothing yet in print) concerning *Lodges, Regulations, Charges, Secrets,* and *Usages,* particularly one written by Mr. *Nicholas Stone,* the Warden of *Inigo Jones,* some of which were too hastily burnt, to prevent their falling into *strange* Hands.

And on *Lady-Day,* 1721, GRAND-MASTER PAYNE proposed for his Successor, our most *Noble Brother* JOHN *Duke* of *Montague, Master* of a *Lodge* ; who, on the 24th of *June* following (when the GRAND FEAST, for the first time was held at *Stationers-Hall*) was proclaimed GRAND-MASTER, on which Day the noble PHILIP *Lord Stanhope* was made a MASON.

Thus by the *Fervency* and *Zeal* of GRAND MASTER PAYNE, the *Freedom* of this Society has been fixed upon a noble and solid

Basis,

Baſis, having this Year produced the *General Regulations,* which he had compiled from the ancient *Uſages* and *Records* of the *Fraternity,* and by whoſe Means a Series of ſuch *noble Perſonages* have preſided at their Head, which no *Age, Society,* or *Nation,* could ever boaſt of.

From hence it appears, that the CRAFT was not in that State of Inactivity, as this *pretended Ancient Maſon* would inſinuate, neither is it to be ſuppoſed, that MASONRY was ſo much forgotten as to render it neceſſary to ſubſtitute any thing *new* in its ſtead, as the *London Lodges* (which were never reduced to a leſs Number than four) ſtill continued their Meetings, and though they were a little Time without an *acting* GRAND-MASTER, I ſuppoſe they were as capable of preſerving the ancient *Traditions, &c.* of the CRAFT, as the Brethren at * *York,* whoſe Numbers were certainly excelled by thoſe at *London,* as the building of ſuch a noble *Edifice* as St. *Paul's,* and other great Works carrying on at that Time, brought MASONS, not only from moſt Parts of *England,* but from ſeveral foreign *Countries.*

D   And

* I ſhould be glad to know how many Lodges there were then at *York.*

And it is certain, that the *Lodges* at *York* approved the Conduct of thofe at *London*, in the Choice of a Grand-Master, &c. fince we have no Account of *their* choofing one, neither have we heard of their having a Grand-Master of their own, till of late Years, when fome Brethren of *Ireland*, who affect Singularity, being refufed the Countenance of their own Grand-Master, and for other Reafons too well known, were glad to affume the Title of *Ancient York Mafons*, and under that Character, have influenced fome *Noble* Brethren (whom we may reafonably conclude have taken no Pains to examine into thefe Particulars) to prefide over them; it is however very clear, that thofe *Noblemen*, have been acknowledged as Grand-Masters, under the *Rofe* only, to prevent giving Offence to the Grand-Master of *England*, for Mr. *Dermott* has dedicated the firft Edition of his *pirated Conftitution-Book* to the *Earl* of *Bleffington*, not as Grand-Master of *Ancient*, *York*, *Scotch*, or *Irifh Mafons* (but as to a *Noble* Brother only) which he would certainly have done (as it would have been a great Honor to them) had he been permitted.

And

And notwithſtanding his Aſſertion, that the *Lodges* in the Country, particularly in *Scotland* and at *York*, kept up their ancient Formalities, Cuſtoms and Uſages, without Alteration, Adding, or Diminiſhing, to this Hour (from whence he concludes them to be the *moſt* Ancient.) It muſt be acknowledged, that as MASONRY muſt not be written, and has been handed down by *oral* Tradition only, for ſo many Ages, that it doubtleſs has received ſeveral Alterations, according to the *Cuſtoms* and *Manners* of the ſeveral *Countries* it has paſſed through, and I am ſure, that every ingenuous MASON, both *Ancient* and *Modern* (Terms which I am obliged to uſe to be underſtood) will likewiſe acknowledge that MASONRY in general has received no little Alteration within theſe twenty Years, though the old *Land-marks* are neverthelefs preſerved.

The *London* MASONS are much beholden to this *faithful* Brother (as he is pleaſed to call himſelf) for his *curious* Account- of his, and *their Society*, particularly of the *modern* Manner of making *Maſons*, with *Boots*, *Spurs*, *Sword* and *Spectacles* on, and their *Aprons* reverſed ; but as the contrary is no-

toriouſly

toriously known, by Masons of all Denominations, it requires no Answer.

His next Assertion is, that they seized on
the Company of *operative Masons* Arms, and
used them as their own.   In Opposition to
which, I shall insert a Paragraph from an
old Record of *Masons*, which says, " The
" Company of MASONS, otherwise termed
" FREE-MASONS, of auncient Staunding,
" and good Reckonning, by Means of affa-
" ble and kind Meetings diverse Tymes,
" and as a loving Brotherhood should use
" to doe, did frequent this mutual *Assembly*
" in the Tyme of King *Henry* the *fifth,* the
" 12th Year of his *most gracious* Reign."
And as the said Record describes a *Coat* of
Arms, much the same with *That* of the
LONDON COMPANY of MASONS, it is generally believed that the said *Company* is de-
scended from the ancient *Fraternity* ; and
consequently bore the same Arms ; and that
in former Times no Man was made *Free*
of that *Company,* till he was made a FREE
and ACCEPTED MASON, as a necesary
Qualification. This, I presume, will sufficiently prove, that the *modern* MASONS
(as he calls them) did not *seize* on the *ope-*
rative Masons Arms (which *he* says is one of
                                           ·the

the Innovations they made) in the Reign of
King *George* the *first*.

But this is done with a View to create a
Belief, that the Arms in the upper Part of the
Frontispiece of his *Book*, is the *Arms* of the
Fraternity, and in order to acquaint us that
he has some Knowledge of *Heraldry*, he has
described them in the following manner.
" In the first Quarter *Azure* a *Lion* ram-
" pant *Or* ; in the second Quarter *Or*, an
" *Ox* passant *sable* ; in the third Quarter *Or*,
" a *Man* with his *Hands* erect, proper robed,
" *Crimson* and *Ermin* ; in the fourth Quar-
" ter *Azure*, an *Eagle* display'd, *Or*. *Crest*,
" the holy *Ark* of the *Covenant*, proper,
" supported by *Cherubims*. Motto, *Kodes la*
" *Adonai, i. e. Holiness to the Lord*." And
having told us what the Prophet *Ezekiel*, the
learned *Spencer*, and *Bochart*, say concerning them, he tells us that they were found in
the Collection of the learned *Hebrewist Arch-
itect* and *Brother*, Rabi *Jacob Jehudah Leon*,
who had formed a *Model* of *Solomon's Temple*,
at the Request of the *States* of *Holland*, in
order to build a *Temple* there, but the Expence being thought too great, it was laid
aside. The *Model*, he says, was afterwards
exhibited

exhibited to publick View at *Paris* and
Vienna, and afterwards in *London*; when
That Rabbi publifhed a Defcription of the
Tabernacle and *Temple*, and dedicated it to
King *Charles* the *Second*; and in the Years
1759 and 1760, he tells us that *he* examined
both thofe Curiofities. This is, to be fure,
an *amazing Proof* of the Authenticity of
thofe *Arms!* but it is ftill more wonderful,
that thofe *very Ancient Mafons*, who are faid
to be fo *extraordinary* cunning, fhould have
no Account of them, till Mr. *Dermott* produced them in Print!

Our *Ancient Mafon* feems highly difpleafed
at a *great* Sword, which, he fays, is placed
before the *Mafter's* Chair in a Lodge, in his
Neighbourhood.

This I fhall likewife venture to pronounce
a notorious Falfehood, unlefs he means the
Quarterly Communication, or GRAND-LODGE,
where a very fuperb * SWORD of *State* is
always

* The prefent SWORD of *State* was a Prefent from
his Grace the Duke of *Norfolk*, while he was GRAND
MASTER, in the Year 1731, being then at *Venice.*
It had been the *Old Trufty* SWORD of GUSTAVUS
ADOLPHUS, King of *Sweden*, and was likewife wore
by

always carried before, and placed by the GRAND-MASTER, as a Token of his great *Authority* and *Power*, and not as an Inſtrument of *War* and *Bloodſhed*, as *he* inſinuates, as *that* is always confined to the Door of the GRAND, as well as of the *particular* Lodges. But the Word GRAND ſtuck in our Author's Throat, and the bringing it out would have been too great an Acknowledgment for him who is *called* GRAND-SECRETARY to *that* Society, which *(he ſays)* is *more* Ancient than *that* which has ever been acknowledged to be the *moſt* Ancient.

The *little* Piece of *Wit*, concerning the *Tyler's* drawing two *Sign-Poſts*, and writing *Jamaica* Rum upon one, and *Barbadoes* Rum upon the other, is (like many other of his *ridiculous* Criticiſms, which I have purpoſely omitted) beneath my Notice. But after his having deviated from the Character of a *Gentleman*, and a MASON, by traducing and treating

by his Succeſſor in War, the brave BERNARD, Duke of *Sax-weimar*, and has both their *Names* on the Blade. The Scabbard is richly adorned with the *Arms* of NORFOLK, and the MASONS *Arms*, in Silver gilt, and ſeveral Hieroglyphics in *Maſonry*. The Croſs at the Hilt repreſents two Columns of the *Corinthian Order*, made of maſſy Silver, and richly gilt.

treating with all the *Redicule* and *Comtempt* be is Master of, the most *respectable Society* perhaps existing, he says, that there are several other *unconstitutional* Proceedings among them, which he passes over in Silence, to avoid giving Offence ; by which, some would think, that his *Modesty* had got the better of his *Intentions,* but as *that* is an *Ingredient* which is not to be found in his *Composition,* we will rather suppose that he had already advanced more than he could well support, and was therefore unwilling to subject himself to any further *Censure.*

Thus we see how much we are beholden to (*him* who concludes himself)

Our most sincere Friend,

Obedient Servant,

And faithful Brother,

LAURENCE DERMOTT.

Notwithstanding his *Sneers* on the *History* of MASONRY, he has quoted some things which require a regular *Historical Account,* to set them in a clear Light ; and though he has contemptuously treated, and refused

the

the Affiftance of feveral *Authors* who have wrote on the Subject of *Mafonry*, he has neverthelefs thought proper to quote Dr. *D'Affigny* (which was one of them) in Defence of the *Royal Arch Mafons*.

He has likewife (to ufe his own Expreffion) *feized* on the *Englifh* MASONS *Old Charges*, their *fhort Charge*, their manner of *conftituting a Lodge*, and their *General Regulations*, both *old* and *new*, and has inferted them in his Book almoft verbatim, except a few Words, and Expreffions, which he has altered, in order to bring them nearer his own Defign. To which he has added the *Regulations* of the *Committee* of *Charity*, as practifed by the *Grand Lodge* in *Ireland* fince the Year 1738, and alfo the *Regulations of* the *York*, or *Ancient Mafons Committee* of *Charity*, as practifed by them fince the Year 1751. With thefe, and a great Number of *Songs* (which make one Half his *Volume*) he has patched up his *Conftitution-Book*, to the great Joy of his *ancient* Brethren, and to *his* (no *fmall*) Advantage, as it is publifhed for his *own* private Emolument, and not for the Benefit of the *Ancient Mafons* Fund, though he is fo *feemingly* folicitous about their Welfare. E If

If our *Author* ſhould aſſert that the *old Charges*, the *Manner of Conſtituting a Lodge*, and the *General Regulations*, which he has publiſhed, are likewiſe the ſame as practiſed in *Ireland*, and by the *Ancient* or *York Ma-ſons*; let it be replyed, that the Brethren of *Ireland*, having obſerved, that from the Foundation of *Maſonry* in that *Kingdom*, it had continued in a fluctuating *State*, were at laſt determined (in Imitation of their Brethren of *England*) to chooſe a *Noble* GRAND-MASTER, and in the Year 1730, they elected JAMES KING, *Lord Viſcount Kingſton*, to that Office, who the Year before had been GRAND-MASTER of the *En-gliſh* MASONS, and who introduced the ſame *Conſtitutions*, and *ancient Uſages*, to the GRAND-LODGE of *Ireland*, which are re-corded in the *Engliſh* MASONS *Conſtitution-Book*.

With Regard to the *ancient* or *York Ma-ſons*, we have no *Regulations* of theirs in Print, but what Mr. *Dermott* has produced, and calls by that Name, and *thoſe* of no longer ſtanding than the Year 1751, which was about the Time that thoſe *very ancient Maſons* began to be much talked of.   From hence

hence is appears that the Masons at *York* approved of the *London* Masons printing the *Conſtitution-Book*, from the ancient Records of the *Fraternity*, in the Year 1723, by *their* not printing one in Oppoſition to it ; and they doubtleſs approved of their Choice of Mr. *Sayer*, as Grand-Master, in the Year 1717, in the room of Sir *Chriſtopher Wren*, or they would certainly have choſen one themſelves.

I cannot help obſerving, that Mr. *Dermott* has not compiled his Book for the Uſe of *Maſons* only, but alſo for ſuch as may be inclined to be initiated into their *Myſteries,* whom he aſſures (in order to draw them into his *Society) that he has made* Free Masonry (both *Ancient* and *Modern) his conſtant Study for twenty Years paſt,* and therefore they may depend on him as a *faithful Guide.* However, I find that his Memory is very ſhort (from which ſome would infer that he is a great *Wit)* and that he is as ſubject to Error as his *Holineſs,* for in *Page* 24, he ſays, that he was made a *Modern Maſon* not above 16 or 17 Years ago ; and in *Page* 2, he aſſerts, that *Maſonry Diſſected,* was publiſhed ſince the firſt *Edition* of his

Book, which I deny, as it is about 40 Years ſince that *Publication,* and I had the Curioſity to buy one myſelf, at leaſt 18 Years ago.

Having finiſhed my *Remarks* on AHIMAN REZON, as well as my *Defence* of our MOST ANCIENT and HONOURABLE FRATERNITY; I ſhall give a brief Account of the *Characters, Principles* and *Practices,* of thoſe who are called *Ancient Maſons,* and conclude with a *Word* of *Advice* to thoſe who are ſtigmatized with the Name of *Moderns.*

Though there are ſeveral Perſons of Character and Ability among the *Ancient Maſons,* the greater Part of them are a ſet of *illeterate* and *mean* Perſons, ſuch as *Chairmen, Porters, Walking Poulterers,* and the like, chiefly Natives of *Ireland,* who finding it not *convenient* to ſtay in their own Country, have fled hither to get an HONEST Livelihood; they herd together at Hedge-Alehouſes, and becauſe they know the *Engliſh* GRAND-LODGE will not authorize their *illicit* and *ignorant* Proceedings, and that the GRAND-MASTER of *Ireland* will not countenance them

them *here*, they have, with the Affiftance of fome HONEST *Yorkfhire-Men*, who have come to *London* on the fame Account, trumpt up what *they* call *Ancient* or *York Mafonry*, and under the fpecious Pretence of being the *moft* Ancient, have drawn in feveral *well meaning* and *worthy* Perfons, by whofe Affiftance and Application, a noble *Peer* has condefcended to permit them to make ufe of his Name, as their *Grand-Mafter*, though (as I obferved before) he feldom, if ever, prefides in any of their *Affemblies*.

Their Initiation *Fee* is, in general, fmall, *viz.* ten *Shillings*, and I can fafely declare, on the WORD of a MASON (which Expreffion I fhall ever hold facred) that I have known their *Mafters* of *Lodges*, many times, to take Notes of Hand, of the new *Members*, for Half that *Fee*, on Account of their extreme Poverty; notwithftanding Mr. *Dermott's* Affertion, that their *Fee* is never lefs than two *Guineas*; and it is no uncommon thing for many of them to come to their *Lodges*, without a Farthing in their *Pockets*, and to borrow as much as will make up a *Sixpenny* Reckoning of three or four different *Members*. Nay, they go ftill farther, for if any of
them

them happen to be *Pennyless,* as they walk the Street, which (I prefume) is often the Cafe, they, without any Ceremony, give the *Sign* or *Signal* of Diftrefs to the firft *Brother* they chance to meet, who is obliged to anfwer, and affift them, or be deemed unworthy their *Vocation.*

Their Contributions to their *Charity* are not *voluntary,* but *obligatory,* and every *Member* of a *Lodge* is obliged to contribute monthly or weekly, a fmall Sum, after the manner of a *petty Box-Club,* or the *Ancient-Mafons* can have no *Charity* for *them.*

The manner of their *working* the *Lodge* is as abfurd, as it is prolix. The firft time I ever went among them was out of Curiofity, and a *Friend* of mine introduced me, without paying any Regard to that *idle* Diftinction between *Ancient* and *Modern.* My *Friend,* and two or three more of the Company were reputable *Tradefmen,* the reft were chiefly fuch *Perfons* as before mentioned. I patiently fat near three Hours, while a redhot *Hibernian* in the *Chair,* was delivering the firft *Lecture* (happy was it for him that my Friend *George Alexander Stevens* was

not

not there, as his *Worship*'s Head would certainly have been *Lectured* on at the *Hay-Market*, and I am of Opinion, that it would have afforded as much *humourous* Matter as any Head in *Stephens*'s Collection.)

Having sat a great While without opening my Lips, except now and then to moisten them with a little *Porter*, which is their constant, and favourite *Liquor*, I at last was Witness to *their* Form of *initiating* a *Member*, who was by Profession a *Chairman*. This Man paid five *Shillings*, and gave a Note of Hand to the *Master* for five more.

I could not help, though a *Stranger*, expressing my Abhorrence of such ridiculous, mean, and scandalous *Practices*, but my *Mouth* was soon stopt by the *Master*, who said, " *Upon my Shoul now, but I believe he* " *is a Modern!*" then turning to me with an Air of *vast* Consequence, but seemingly much vext, " *Sir*, said he, *the Devil burn* " *me, but I believe you are a Modern-Mason,* " *and that's as good as being no Mason at all!*" Having uttered this, they all cried out, with Voices hoarse as *Thunder*, for the Space of five Minutes, *Hobligate him, Hobligate him*; which *Ceremony* I was obliged to submit to,

as

as I now began to think my *Life* in Danger, and glad was I, when I had got out of the *House*. But I have since that, gained Admittance into several of their *Lodges*, from the same Motive of Curiosity, and shall ever be ready to acquaint any regular *Mason* with their *Customs* and *Ceremonies*.

The manner of their *Funeral Processions* is a Disgrace to *Society*. I once saw one which went from *Tower-hill* to *St. Pancras*; the *Corpse* was borne all the Way by sturdy *Chairmen*, who now and then stopt, while others took their Places; about 200 *Persons*, cloathed as *Masons*, attended, some in *laced* Waistcoats, some in *Military* Uniforms, and others with scarcely a *Coat* or *Shirt* to their *Backs*; who having sat in *Ale-houses* adjacent to where the *Corpse* lay, for three or four Hours before, hooting and hollooing with the Windows open, to the great Disturbance of the Neighbourhood, and the Scandal of Masonry; many of them were at last so inebriated, that they required almost as much supporting as their deceased Brother; and Countryman, which afforded much Sport and Diversion to several Hundreds of *Spectators*, who had assembled on that Occasion.

To

TO THE REGULAR MASONS OF ENGLAND.

Dear Brethren,

HAving given you a true *Portrait* of thofe *Deceivers*, and falfe *Brethren*, I hope you will ufe your utmoft Endeavours to guard againft all their *Innovations*, illicit, irregular, and ridiculous *Forms* and *Ceremonies*, *holding faft the Form of found Words, without wavering.* Let not the *Mafters* of *Lodges* fuffer any of their *Brethren* to become Members with thofe *fham* Ancients, as their *Lodges, &c.* are deemed *irregular* by our Laws, and all who affift at *Makings* in *irregular Lodges*, or attend *Mafons* Funerals, *cloathed* as fuch, without a fpecial Licence, are fubject to the following Cenfure of the GRAND LODGE, *viz.* That they fhall not be *Grand-Officers*, or *Officers of particular Lodges*, nor admitted into *Lodges*, even as *Vifitors*. They fhall likewife be rendered incapable of *Tyling*, or attending on a *Lodge*, or partaking of the *general Charity*, if they come to want it.

If any Perfon, whom thefe pretended *Ancients* have drawn in, finds that he is im-

F   pofed

pofed on, and applies to a *regular Lodge* to be *initiated*, I think there can be no Harm in *re-making* him *gratis*, provided he is a Perfon of *Character*, and has paid the accuftomed *Fee* before, and will faithfully promife not to attend fuch *irregular Meetings* again   This Opinion however, is fubmitted to the Senfe of the GRAND LODGE.

It were much to be wifhed, that the *Mafters* of *Lodges* were more *brief* in their Inftructions than they commonly are, efpecially when there is *Bufinefs* of another Nature, which takes up much Time; as by keeping the *Lodge* open too long, the *Brethren* are detained from their *Families*, which brings Difgrace upon the *Fraternity*; for, a *Lodge* is a Place of pleafant Relaxation from intenfe *Study*, or Hurry of *Bufinefs*, and therefore Prolixity fhould be avoided; befides, every one who is made a *Mafon*, has not a Memory to retain every Particular contained in long *Lectures*, and therefore difpair of ever making any tolerable Figure in the *Craft*, and often neglect the *Fraternity* for ever after on that Account.

As *Ignorance* and *Immorality* are the greateſt Enemies to every well regulated *Society*, it is hoped that the MASONS will be particularly careful that the Perſons they admit, are ſuch as our excellent *Conſtitutions* require, for the Preſervation of *Harmony* within the *Lodges*, as well as their *Reputation* without.

If what I have written proves of the leaſt Service to that Society, of which I have long been an unworthy Member, my Expectations will be ſufficiently anſwered. And as I commenced *Author* merely by Accident, and drew my *Pen* in a good *Cauſe*, I hope the candid and judicious *Brethren*, will excuſe whatever *Inaccuracies* and *Improprieties* may appear, for I can aſſure them (*on the Word of a Maſon*) that I deſire the Reputation of an *Author*, as little as I merit it.

A

COLLECTION

O F

MASONS ODES and SONGS.

Moſt of them entirely new.

An ODE for three Voices, and a thorough
Baſs for the Harpſichord.

The Words by Brother H. JACKSON, the
Muſic by Brother GILDING.

1.

TRIO.

WAKE the Lute and quiv'ring Strings,
  Myſtic Truths URANIA brings;
Friendly Viſitant, to Thee
We owe the Depths of MASONRY:
Faireſt of the Virgin Choir,
Warbling to the golden Lyre,
Welcome, here thy ART prevail:
Hail! divine URANIA, hail!

2.

SOLO.

Here in FRIENDSHIP's ſacred *Bow'r*,
The downy wing'd, and ſmiling Hour,
Mirth invites, and ſocial Song,
Nameleſs *Myſteries* among.

DUETTO

DUETTO and TRIO.

Crown the Bowl and fill the Glaſs,
To ev'ry Virtue, ev'ry Grace,
To the BROTHERHOOD reſound,
Health, and let it *thrice* go round.

3.

DUETTO.

We reſtore the Times of old,
The blooming, glorious Age of Gold ;
As the new Creation free,
Bleſt with gay EUPHROSINE ;
We with Godlike Science talk,
And with fair ASTREA walk ;
INNOCENCE adorns the Day,
Brighter than the Smiles of *May.*

4.

TRIO and SOLO.

Pour the roſy Wine again,
Wake a louder, louder Strain ;
Rapid ZEPHYRS, as ye fly,
Waft our Voices to the Sky,
While we celebrate the NINE,
And the Wonders of the TRINE ;
While the ANGELS ſing above,
As we below of PEACE and LOVE.

The Muſic of the above favourite ODE, in Score, to be had of Brother *Gilding* in *Alderſgate-ſtreet,* near *Long-lane.*

An

An ODE facred to MASONRY.

The Words by Brother J. G. and R. M.

The Mufic for four Voices and a thorough Bafs, by Dr. HAYES.

DUETTO.

COMUS away with all thy revel Train,
    Begone ye Loud, ye Wanton, and ye Vain.
Come, penfive SCIENCE, bring with thee,
COMMERCE, and ARTS, and INDUSTRY.

TRIO.

Patriot VIRTUE alfo bring,
And LOYALTY who loves his KING;
Sweet PEACE thy Footfteps hither bend,
And LIBERTY, the MUSES Friend.

DUETTO and QUARTETTO.

HONOR and INNOCENCE come here,
Strangers to Flatt'ry and to Fear;
Let facred TRUTH too join the Band,
JUSTICE and MERCY Hand in Hand.

RECITATIVE.

But chiefly thou fair FRIENDSHIP, welcome Gueft,
And HARMONY to crown the Mafon's Feaft.

CHORUS.

Hail MASONRY! thou faithful, kind
Inftructor of the Human Mind;
Thy focial Influence extends
Beyond the narrow Sphere of Friends;
Thy Harmony and Truth improve
On Earth our univerfal LOVE.

SONG

SONG for three VOICES.

The Words by Brother J. THOMAS.
The Music by Brother ORME.   Both of *Chester*.
Or to the Tune of *By Jove I'll be free*.

TRIO.

ARISE, gentle MUSE, and thy *Wisdom* impart,
To each *Bosom* that glows with the Love of our ART,
For the Bliss that from thy Inspiration accrues,
Is what all should admire, and each MASON pursues.

CHORUS.

Hence *Harmony* springs, 'tis the Cement of *Love*,
Fair *Freedom* on Earth, and bright *Union* above.

TRIO.

Tho' *Malice* our Joy shou'd attempt to controul,
Tho' *Discord* around like an Ocean shou'd roll ;
To the one we'll be deaf, to the other be blind,
For *Wisdom* alone is the *Strength* of the Mind.

CHORUS. Hence *Harmony* springs, &c.

TRIO.

The bright Charms of *Beauty* for ever will shine,
Our ART to adorn with a Lustre divine ;
'Till Time circling round shall unfold the great Truth,
Which thus has united the Sage and the Youth.

CHORUS. Hence *Harmony* springs, &c.

The MYSTIC BOWER.

A SONG for three VOICES.

The Music by Dr. BOYCE.

'TIS to MASONS ever pleasing,
In the MYSTIC BOW'R to meet ;
Temp'rate *Wine* their Joys increasing,
Joys which *Music* makes complete.

When

When with Wine our Veins are fwelling,
Friendship's Fires the brighter burn;
Mufic, Grief and Care expelling,
Bids true Joy fucceed in Turn.

They fay that fuch *Pleafures* fhou'd not be conceal'd,
Let *Fools* their Ill-Nature and Envy expofe;
We laugh at their Folly, be nothing reveal'd,
Our *Pleafures* will always be under the Rose.

A SONG for three Voices.

The Mufic by Brother Orme.

I.

GUardian Genius of our Art divine,
   Unto thy faithful *Sons* appear;
Ceafe now o'er Ruins of the Eaft to pine,
And fmile on blooming Beauties here.

2.

Egypt, *Syria*, and proud *Babylon*,
No more thy blifsful Prefence claim;
In *England* fix thy ever-during Throne,
Where Myriads do confefs thy Name.

3.

The *Sciences* from Eaftern Regions brought,
Which after fhewn in *Greece* and *Rome*,
Are here in many ftately Lodges taught,
To which remoteft Brethren come.

4.

Behold what *Strength* our rifing Domes uprears,
Till mixing with the Azure Skies;
Behold what *Beauty* thro' the Whole appears,
So wifely built they muft furprize.

Nor

5.

Nor are we only to thefe Arts confin'd,
For we the Paths of Virtue trace;
By us Man's rugged Nature is refin'd,
And polifh'd into Love and Peace.

N. B. The Mufic of the laft Ode, and three Songs,
to be had of Brother *Thomas Hale*, Schoolmafter at
Darnhall, Chefhire; or of Mr. *Butler*, Bookfeller, the
Corner of *Paternofter-row, Cheapfide.*

SONG by Brother H. JACKSON.

Tune, *By Jove I'll be free.*

I.

BEGIN, O ye Mufes, a FREE-MASONS Strain;
    Let the Numbers be gentle, and eafy, and plain,
Tho' fometimes in Concert fublimely we fing,
While each *Brother* MASON joins Hands with a KING;
For PRINCES difdain not Companions to be,
With the Man that is own'd for a MASON and free.

2.

Why feek our beft Nobles our *Myft'ry* to know,
And rather fing here than fip Tea with a Beau?
The fweet Notes of *Knowledge* more pow'rfully call,
Than a Fav'rite at Court, or a Toaft at the Ball;
For Truth's fake a Lord is of equal Degree,
With a Man that is own'd for a MASON and free.

3.

'Twas HEAVEN firft lighted the glorious Flame
Of SCIENCE, that Sages FREE-MASONRY name;
From *Adam* it flow'd to the Pat'archs of old,
The wife KING prefer'd it to Ophirs of Gold;
And HIRAM of TYRE join'd with him to be
Of the Number of thofe who were MASONS and free.

G   The

4.

The faireſt Proportion of Things we diſcry,
With the deep *Geometrician's* and *Moraliſt's* Eye;
The Records of Time from all others conceal'd,
Like Leaves of the *Sybils* to us are reveal'd;
What's more! we in BROTHERLY LOVE all agree,
With the Man that is own'd for a MASON and free.

5.

The Wiſdom of *Greece,* and old *Rome* we explore,
Nay paſs to the Learn'd of the *Memphian* Shore;
What Secrets *Euphrates* and *Tygris* have known,
And *Paleſtine* gather'd are here made our own:
Well may the World wonder what ſtrange things we ſee
With the Man that is own'd for a MASON and free.

6.

The *Gregs, Antigallics,* and others, they ſay,
Have ſet up their *Lodges,* and mimic our Way,
But Frogs claim a Curſe when they croak from the Fen,
And Monkies a Kick when they imitate Men;
In vain, ſhallow Mortals, you Rivals would be,
To the Man that is own'd for a MASON and free.

7.

Tho' the Fair from our Rights are for ever debar'd,
Ah! *Ladies* repine not, nor cenſure too hard,
You have no Rivals here, not ev'n in the Glaſs,
Where *Fribbles* ſo doat on the Shade of an Aſs;
Your own deareſt *Pictures,* our *Hearts* could you ſee,
Would be found in the Man that's a MASON and free.

8.

The brighteſt of *Graces,* and *Virtues* here join,
No ſuch *Angel-looks* in the Drawing-Room ſhine;

Bleſt

Bleſt *Concord*, and Eagle-ey'd *Truth* hover round,
And fair *Faith* and *Friendſhip* bid ſee the Bowl crown'd;
Here's a Health, let it paſs with the Number of III,
To the Man that is own'd for a MASON and free.

N. B. The above Song being printed in an imperfect
and execrable Manner, in Mr. DERMOTT's Collection,
is the Occaſion of its being reprinted in this.

The LODGE deſcrib'd,

By Brother BRICE, of *Exeter*.

Tune, *O the Roaſt Beef, &c.*

1.

WHEN a LODGE, juſt and perfect, is form'd all
      aright,
The *Sun-beams* cœleſtial (although it be Night)
Refulgent and glorious appear to the Sight
    Of hearty and faithful true MASONS,
Cho.   True MASONS in *Heart, Word* and *Deed.*

2.

Their *Eaſtern* mild RULER then lays the firſt Stone,
The *Craftſmen*, obedient, united as one,
Him copy, and cheerfully work till high Noon,
    As hearty and faithful true MASONS, *&c.*

3.

Rough *Aſhler* they hew, and form by the *Square*,
By the *Level* lay *Solids*, and by the *Plumb* rear
Their Uprights; *Strength beautiful* being the Care
    Of hearty and faithful true MASONS, *&c.*

4.

Hence a Building, by *Wiſdom* contriv'd, does ariſe,
Founded in the *Center*, ſublime, to the *Skies*,
Which Storms, Thunder, War, and Time's Envy defies,
    Bleſt Labour of faithful true MASONS, *&c.*

G 2   Strong

5.

Strong *Net-work* they carve — (its Emblem they know)
Where *Lillies*, Milk-white, and rich *Fruit* seem to grow;
Concord, Peace, and Plenty; — How lovely the Show
    To all hearty and faithful true MASONS, &c.

6.

No *Babel* Diftraction is heard, no Debate,
The *Cock's* Crow they need not, the *Dog's* Barking hate,
Decorum they keep, and avoid idle Prate,
    Being hearty and faithful true MASONS, &c.

7.

Intent on their Task, their Labour's their Pleasure;
Nor seems it, however prolong'd, beyond Measure;
But all appear tir'd most—when most at Leisure,
    Such trusty true Workmen are MASONS, &c.

8.

When dismist, Wages paid, and all satisfy'd,
As loth to depart, they yet social abide,
Join Hands, with join'd Hearts, toasting—Joy e'er betide,
    All hearty and faithful true MASONS, &c.

9.

Then, *Brothers* well met, — charge right, and let's sing
Like ourselves, trebly thrice *To the* CRAFT *and the* KING,
And crowning III Cheers, make the happy LODGE ring,
    Proclaiming us happy true MASONS,
  Cho.   True MASONS in Heart, Word and Deed.

The FREE-MASONS Toasts, a SONG,

By Brother BRICE.

Tune, *Of noble Race was Shinkin.*

1.

COME, now, lov'd loving *Brothers,*
  Since serious Work is ended,
    Let Wine give Birth
    To social Mirth,
With tuneful Songs attended.

                      Charge,

2.

Charge, then, with Liquid Powder,
Each his found-bottom'd *Bumper* ;
 As to the KING,
 And CRAFT we sing,
It should be with a *Thumper*.

3.

Off with it, clap, huzza! Boys,
As do our Rites require,
 Thrice III make III, III, III,
 Mind Discipline,
And all as one give Fire.

4.

Again replenish'd high, Lads,
To our Worshipful GRAND-MASTER,
 And *Wardens* two,
 Our next Toast's due :
Heav'n shield them from Disaster.

5.

Next to all worthy MASONS,
Howe'er by Fortune batter'd,
 And poor as *Job*,
 Where, o'er the Globe,
Them Providence hath scatter'd.

6.

And, as the *Fair Sex* ever
By MASONS are adored,
 Health to their Charms,
 In MASONS Arms
Who lig in Love assured.

The

The WARDENS *Song*, at closing the LODGE.

The Words by Brother RILEY.

Tune, *As Calms appear when Storms are past.* In Alfred.

1.

THE *Sun* is set, the LODGE is clos'd,
   And we our WORK have done:
Then BRETHREN let us all rejoice
   To see the setting *Sun.*

2.

Bright PHOEBUS in his gilded Car,
   His daily Course has run:
And we have finish'd quite complete,
   By setting of the *Sun.*

3.

Then since we have perform'd with Care,
   The WORK which we begun;
Let ev'ry MASON take his Glass
   At setting of the *Sun.*

4.

With FRIENDSHIP, MIRTH and INNOCENCE,
   We will be all as one;
And spend a joyous Hour or two,
   At setting of the *Sun.*

5.

We'll banish *Dullness* far from hence,
   And *Discord* we will shun;
That they may not disturb our Cheer
   At setting of the *Sun.*

6.

Like PHOEBUS to his THETIS' Arms,
   (When these our Joys are done)
We'll fly unto our SISTERS Charms,
   'Till rising of the *Sun.*

But

7.

But firſt in *myſtic* Form we'll drink,
  E'er we proceed to Fun;
And thank our MASTER for his Care
  'Till ſetting of the *Sun.*

The Character of a MASON.

The Words by Brother R ɪ ʟ ᴇ ʏ.

Tune, *The Big-Belly'd Bottle.*

I.

ALL you that would know what a MASON muſt be,
  A while give Attention and liſten to me;
I promiſe that I'll not detain you too long,
But his *Character* briefly ſum up in a Song.

2.

The *moral* Law he by his Tenure muſt keep,
Be likewiſe well ſkill'd in our MYST'RIES ſo deep;
For if with the ART well acquainted is he,
Nor ATHEIST, nor LIBERTINE he'll ever be.

3.

He's a peaceable *Subject* wherever he works,
Conſpiracy never within his Breaſt lurks;
He's loyal, he's honeſt, he's true to his Word,
Which makes him Companion for KING, DUKE or LORD.

4.

He's a good Man and true, and he acts on the *Square,*
He lives within *Compaſs,* he's juſt to the Fair;
Immoral and ſcandalous Men are refus'd,
That our *Laws* and *Traditions* may not be abus'd.

5.

He's taught by our ART *not to do his own Will,*
But his Paſſions ſubdue, like a CRAFTSMAN of Skill;
The Preferment he gains to his Merit is due,
If by Chance he is one of th'*intelligent* few.

Tho'

6.

Tho' a MASON is FELLOW and BROTHER to KINGS,
What levels *them* moſt to *them* moſt *Honor* brings;
And the Deference which th'*Inferior* gives,
The *Superior* with modeſt Reluĉtance receives.

7.

A MASONS *Tongue* hangs in a BROTHER's Defence,
With *Topics* improper it ne'er gives Offence;
In ſhort, if you'd know what a MASON muſt be,
APPLY, be ACCEPTED, and own'd to be FREE.

ADVICE to the LADIES.

The Words by Brother RILEY.

Tune, *Ye Swains that are courting a Maid.*

1.

IT has oft of the *Females* been ſaid,
   (But you'll own the Report is not true)
That they are not FREE-MASONS made,
For they cannot their Paſſions ſubdue;
That they never can ſubjeĉt their Will,
Nor be bound any *Secrets* to keep,
No never can keep their *Tongues* ſtill,
Except when in Bed, faſt aſleep.

2.

See how *common* Fame will tell Lies,
And ſcandalous Stories retail!
But MASONS thoſe always deſpiſe,
Who againſt the Fair Sex dare to rail:
There are ſeveral *Females* renown'd
For Sentiments truly refin'd,
Whoſe Conduĉt is conſtantly found,
By the CRAFT to be juſt, true, and kind.

The

3.

The thrice myftic *Number* of III, III, III,
And the myftical *Number* of III,
The MUSES and GRACES divine,
Are the *Damfels* I mean that are free:
The CARDINAL VIRTUES fo bright,
Who prefide o'er each *principal* SIGN,
And CYNTHIA who governs the Night,
In the LODGES refplendently fhine.

4.

But 'tis not thefe *fair* ones alone,
For INNOCENCE kindly each Night,
Vouchfafes to defcend from her Throne,
To *cloathe* ev'ry MASON in *White:*
There's FAITH, HOPE and CHARITY fair,
Who teach us the *Ladder* to climb,
As, nightly, the *Fabric* we rear,
By INDUSTRY, PATIENCE and TIME.

5.

Then *Ladies* attend to Advice,
And liften to what I impart,
In *Virtue* and *Honor* be nice,
Learn to govern the *Tongue* and the *Heart;*
In fhort you muft copy the *Fair,*
Whom I have juft mention'd before,
And then we will try, I declare,
To admit you within the LODGE Door.

H   The

The three following S O N G S, imitated from the *French*, and adapted to easy *English Tunes*,

By Brother ALEXANDER REID.

Taken from the Almanac dé *Frenc Maçons*, 1758.

CHANSON I.   Air, *Dans nos hamoaux la paix &
l'Innocence.*

1.

DANS nos banquets, sous l'aile du mystére,
   Nous nous livrons á d'innocens plaisirs,
Bien au dessus du stupide Vulgaire ;
C'est la Raison qui regle nos desirs,
Que la Candeur a pris soin de forger.
Au vrai bon heur la Sagesse nous mene,
Et nous vivons sans crainte & sans danger.

2.

Dans ces loisirs que le Prophane blâme,
Nous élevons d'utiles monumens ;
Notre ordre porte en nous un trait de Flame,
Qui fait germer les plus beaux Sentimens.
La Jalousie & la haine étouffées,
Nous enseigneron comment il faut jouir ;
A l'Amitiè nous dressons des trophées,
Que les Vertus prennent soin d'embellir.

CHANSON

SONG I.   Tune, *Give us Glasses my Wench.*

I.

UNDER *Mystery's* Wing,
  We drink and we sing,
And divert us with innocent Mirth ;
While *Reason* presides,
And our Revelry guides,
We're the happiest Mortals on Earth.
For our Candour disdains,
Laying heavier Chains,
Than true Happiness always may bear ;
And while *Wisdom* excites,
All our *mystical Rites,*
We live without Danger or Fear.

2.

In this pleasing Retreat,
While the *Brethren* thus meet,
Let the Vulgar our *Order* abuse ;
Our Maxims inspire,
The true *social* Fire,
And Sentiments noble infuse.
Thus, the Pleasures of Life,
We enjoy without Strife ;
For we Hatred and Jealousy scorn ;
And to FRIENDSHIP's due Praise,
New Trophies we raise,
Which *Virtue* still helps to adorn.

SONG

CHANSON II. Air, *Pour sommeire mon Ame, à*
l'Empire de plaisin.

I.

EN depit de la haine,
 Qu'on a pour nous en tous lieux,
Cherissons notre Chaine,
 Et resserons — en les nœuds.
Sans cesse on nous tympanise,
 On nous lance maint brocard;
Mais souvent qui nous meprise,
 Ne merite aucun regard.

2.

Nous bravons le langage
 De ces fameux beaux esprits;
Aux mœurs du premier âge,
 Nous sommes assujettis.
Une Amitié vive & pure,
 Nous dispense ses faveurs;
Et la voix de la Nature,
 Se fait entendre á nos Cœurs.

3.

On veut nous faire un Crime,
 D'etre trop mysterieux,
L'objet qui nous anime,
 N'a rien que de vertueuse.
Nous goutous en Assurance,
 Le fruit de nos douse loisirs,
Mais un aimable decence
 Ordonne á tous nos plaisirs.

4.

Ici d'un Air affable,
 On se voit, on s'entretient;
On se rend sociable,
 On s'excuse, on se prévient.
Sans haine, & sans jalousie
 Nous sommes toujours unis
Et nous n'avons d'autre envie
 Que de plaire á nos Amis.

APOLOGNE.

Song II. Tune, *An old Woman cloathed in Grey,*

1.

IN spite of the prejudic'd Hate,
 The Vulgar against us retain;
Let us new Attachments create,
 And strengthen each Link of our Chain.
Without ceasing they slander us still,
 And fling at us many a Joke;
But those who of MASONS speak ill,
 Are not worthy our Wrath to provoke.

2.

We challenge the Witty, or Sage,
 Our Morals, or Deeds to gainsay;
Since those of the primitive Age,
 We are bound to esteem and obey.
A *Friendship* that's warm and sincere,
 Does always her Favours dispense;
And our Hearts to be sway'd will appear,
 By the Dictates of Nature and Sense.

3.

Perhaps some may deem it a Fault,
 That we so mysterious are,
But *Virtue* alone we are taught
 Is the Object that's worthy our Care.
Assur'd of being honest, we taste
 This cheerful Amusement at Leisure,
With the Presence of Decency grac'd,
 Which regulates every Pleasure.

4.

Hence it is that we see every BROTHER,
 An affable Air entertain;
And excusing the Faults of each other,
 A *sociable* Spirit maintain.
Without Hatred, or Jealousy, thus
 United we MASONS do live;
And he only is envied by us,
 Who his Friends the most Pleasure can give.

Song

APOLOGNE.

JUpiter un Jour ent en tête
De depecher un Deputé,
Pour aller par tout faire equête
On feroit *la Fidelité*
Seigneur *Mercure* en Meffager habile
Part, & promet au plus puiffant des Dieux,
De bientot decouvrir l'afile,
De *la Deeffe*. Il vient en ces bas Lieux.
Et s'n fut bien vite á Cythere,
S'en informer au Dieu d'Amour
Qui d'abord ne fçavoit quelle reponfe faire
Et qui dit a la fin, J'ignore fon fejour.

Pen content de cette Vifite,
Mercure s'en va chez l'Hymen;
Oh! l'ignorant! Eft ee la qu'elle Habite?

Ne l'ayant paftrové & pourfuivant Chemin
Il crut ne pas perdre fa peine,
En a'llant droit chez l'Amitié;

Mais fon efperance fut vaine:
Son Hoftefle d'un ton trifte á faire pitié
Lui dit, Helas! *la Deeffe* chérie,
Que vous cherchez eft ici rarement;
Mais vous pouvez aller chez la Maçonnerie,
Et vous la trouverez indubitablement.

SONG III. Tune, *Abbot of Canterbury.*

GREAT JUPITER took it one Day in his Head
To send forth a *Meffenger* (as it is faid)
To fearch every where, and ftrictly enquire,
Where the *Goddefs* FIDELITY chofe to retire?
            Derry down, hey derry down.

Nimble *Mercury* ftrait as a Meffenger dreft,
A punctual Obedience to Orders expreft;
And promis'd Great JOVE, he wou'd certainly find
Where fhe was, if with *Deities,* or with *Mankind.*
            Derry down.

Then down hies the *God,* to fam'd *Cythera's* Grove,
In hopes of fome News from the young *God of Love,*
Who at firft could not tell how to make a Reply,
But at laft told the Truth, tho' accuftom'd to lie.
            Derry down.

I'm ignorant, faith, fays the arch little *Unchin,*
What Place for FIDELITY you muft go fearch in,
But am vaftly furpriz'd you fhou'd think *here* to find her,
When you know that my *Mother* and *I* never mind her.
            Derry down.

This Anfwer not fuiting at all to his Tafte,
Away then to *Hymen* does *Mercury* hafte;
But what Ignorance here did he fhew of Mankind!
To imagine FIDELITY *there* he fhould find.
            Derry down.

Difappointed again he continued his Way,
But thought to himfelf, it would caufe no long Stay,
And perhaps it might happen to anfwer his Ends,
If Enquiry he made of the *Goddefs of Friends.*
            Derry Down.

But vain were his Hopes in his Search here likewife,
For his Hoftefs thus anfwer'd with Tears in her Eyes,
Alas, honeft Friend, this GODDESS fo dear!
For whom you enquire, is feldom feen here.
            Derry down.

In one only Place you can find her on Earth,
So haften away to the true Sons of Mirth;
To a LODGE of FREE-MASONS immediate repair,
And no manner of doubt, but you'll meet with her there.
            Derry down, hey derry down.

SONG by Brother C. SMART, A. M.

Tune, *Ye frolickſome Sparks of the Game.*

I.

A MASON is great and reſpected,
　Tho' *Cavillers* wrangle and mock;
His *Plan* is in WISDOM projected,
　His *Edifice* built on a ROCK.
Cho. The Attempts of his *Foes* miſcarry,
　　　And ever in vain are found;
　　Or ſo wide, that they need no Parry,
　　　Or ſo weak, that they make no Wound.

2.

GOOD-NATURE's an *Engliſhman's* Merit,
　A Title all *Britons* deſire;
But *We* claim the *Name* and the *Spirit,*
　From the CORNER-STONE up to the SPIRE.
Cho. The Attempts of our *Foes* miſcarry, *&c.*

3.

Tho' often decry'd and derided,
　No *Tyrant* our *Freedom* controuls,
With us *mighty* MONARCHS have ſided,
　And EMP'ROR's are writ in our ROLLS.
Cho. The Attempts of our *Foes* miſcarry, *&c.*

4.

Then fill up the Glaſs and be funny,
　Attend to due METHOD and FORM;
The *Bee* that can make the moſt *Honey,*
　Is fairly the *Flow'r* of the *Swarm.*
Cho. The Attempts of our *Foes* miſcarry, *&c.*

F I N I S.

A DEFENCE

OF

LAURENCE DERMOTT

AND THE

ANTIENTS.

A DEFENCE OF LAURENCE DERMOTT
AND THE ANTIENTS.

DR. CHETWODE CRAWLEY has made careful
and, I regret to say, fruitless search, for traces
of Laurence Dermott's early life and Irish
Masonic career; but, unfortunately, the leaf of the
Register of the Grand Lodge of Ireland, on which his
name would probably have been recorded, is missing.
To do justice to his merits would require a special
volume. The following brief sketch, however, may not
be without interest.

His name first appears in the Register of the
Antients under date 1st February, 1752. The date of
his initiation is there given as "Jan. 14, 1740-1." The
lodge in which he was made is not clearly stated, but it
was probably No. 26 Dublin, for that lodge is mentioned,
and in that lodge, after having filled several subordinate
offices, he was duly installed in the Master's Chair on
the 24th June, 1746. We have it in his own handwriting
that on the 24th June, 1761, he was "in the forty-first
year of his age."

He was elected Grand Secretary on the 5th February,
1752, after having satisfied his predecessor (John
Morgan) that he was in every respect well qualified for
that office.

At this time he was a painter, and is so registered.
In Grand Lodge on the 13th July, 1753, he stated that
he "was obliged to work twelve hours in the day for
the master painter who employed him."

His remarkable tact, energy, and firmness doubtless
contributed to the improvement of his social position,
for in 1767 he was able to present to the Grand Lodge

a Throne for the Grand Master, for which he had paid £34. In 1769 we find him described as a Wine Merchant, and in this business he appears to have continued until his death in 1791.

He filled the office of Grand Secretary with marked ability until 1771, when he was appointed Deputy Grand Master by the Duke of Athole, on the recommendation of the Grand Lodge. He retired from the office of D.G. Master in 1777, but was reappointed by the Earl of Antrim in 1783. In 1787 he finally resigned, on account of age and infirmities.

The upward progress of the Antients as an organized body may fairly be dated from Dermott's appointment as Grand Secretary. His many services were frequently acknowledged by the Grand Lodge, but the following resolution unanimously passed on the occasion of his resignation of the office of D.G. Master in 1787 will doubtless sufficiently evince the esteem in which he was then held by his brethren :—"That the thanks of the Grand Lodge be given to the R.W. Lau. Dermott, Esq., Past Deputy Grand Master, who after forty-seven years zealously and successfully devoted to the service of the Craft had now retired from the eminent station which he held, and to whose Masonic knowledge and abilities, inflexible adherence to the Ancient Laws of the Fraternity, and impartial administration of Office the Fraternity are so much indebted."

The letter here reproduced is the only one I have seen in the handwriting of Dermott. As will be noted, it is strikingly characteristic, and was written to the members of his favourite Lodge No. 5, now the Albion Lodge, No. 9, London

The following letters were originally published in the *Freemasons' Chronicle*, London, between December, 1888, and April, 1889. As will be seen, they were written in response to "Comments" (by the late Bro. Jacob Norton, of Boston) on "Masonic Facts and Fictions," the criticism being undertaken by him at my particular request, he having previously informed me

Law Dermott's most Respectful Compliments to his good Brethren of N:5 can not attend them this evening.

D— would gladly embrace any Opportunity (consistent with his Duty) to add to the honor or pleasure of Brother Peters Jun.r — having an high esteem for the.se Peters ten.r & Jun.r therefore would rejoice at either of them Joining N:5 — But of this present be only to obtain an immediate In- =stallation &c. such proceeding can not be productive of honor or Utility to any party. The Grand Regulations of Dec.r 4. 1771 (in the Greenbay's p.page.jron) requires the Candidate should be 12 months on our Grand Lodge Registry And (in Installing) chusing of officers at this time is unreasonable and Incurable, because the Warrant expressly says, "Such Installations to be before or near every "St. John's day during the Continuance of this Lodge for ever", this is the condition of the Warrant of which it is needless to say more.

If Bro.r Peters is or on an immediate return to Novascotia his friends here may on a short time Legally grant what we can not give at present without breach of duty. And which if done would be an evil precedent to those who expect (Installing Instructions) Instructions from us.

Bro.r Brother Peters offer'd himself as a member of N:5 at the proper time of Chusing & Installing &c. D— would be one of the first to give every As =Sistance in his power. In the mean time that Sincerity which should ever accompany Duty and real friendship has dictated this Card

Aug 7. 1787.

Mr Joseph Williams, Secy Nº 55

or his substitute ————

Castle Eating house, Castle Court

Cornhill

Mr Downes to 1693. or
Assignment of October Sessions.
1695 ————

that he did not agree with the evidence and opinions expressed in that book.

It is possible that there are, or may be hereafter, others whose ideas coincide with those of my venerable and esteemed friend. I have, therefore, deemed it advisable to revise my answers and give them a place in this volume, in order that they may be pre-served in a more compact form than that in which they first appeared. I have not thought it either desirable or necessary to present Bro. Norton's " Comments " in detail, as the nature of his criticism will doubtless be sufficiently indicated by my replies, and in most cases I have repeated his own words ; but should any of my readers be desirous of perusing them in their entirety. they will be found in the afore-named journal from the 20th October, 1888, to the 16th March, 1889 ·—

1.

8th DECEMBER, 1888.

§EEING that Brother Norton has started a fresh subject in the *Freemasons' Chronicle*, I may fairly assume that for the present he has finished his " Comments " on my recently published work. If that be really so, I am rather sorry, for although our critical brother has been most unsparing in his denunciations of the Antients, and Laurence Dermott in particular, his observations on the contents of the book are like angels' visits, " few and far between." I shall hereafter direct his attention to one or two points on which I particularly wish for his opinion ; but I have first to thank him for having acceded to my request—although contrary to his own inclination —and the simple fact that I am now endeavòuring to answer his arguments should sufficiently evince that I am not in the least offended with him for his inability to agree with me in this matter. He, I am sure, will not take amiss anything I may say in so doing, for while condemning his logic I cannot help admiring his pluck.

I

Being familiar with Brother Norton's views on the subject of the Antients, and also his antipathy to their leader, I felt some little curiosity as to how he would dispose of some of my "facts," although I was not much surprised when he informed me that he was not a convert to my theory; but when I afterwards learnt that he had only read a portion of the book, it seemed to me that he was scarcely doing himself, or even the author, justice in thus expressing a decided opinion on the merits of a theory with which he had only a partial acquaintance. Indeed, it savoured so much of prejudice, and so nearly resembled a verdict of guilty without having heard the evidence, that I strongly urged him to read the book carefully through, and then let me know his views. He says he has now done as I wished, but his opinion is unchanged, and I am bound to believe him, although I must confess to some little doubt as to his having kept in view the adjective in my request. However, assuming that he has given the book a fair amount of attention, his mode of disposing of the facts referred to has evidently been the very common one of shutting his eyes to them—or, at all events, he has not thought them worthy of notice.

After reading Brother Norton's first " Comments," in the *Chronicle*, No. 719, I was forcibly reminded of the practice popularly imputed to gentlemen of the legal profession when they have a weak case to defend, *i.e.*, abuse the plaintiff's witnesses; and having now read the whole of his dissertation, I am of opinion that he has adhered to this practice most assiduously. Probably my inexperience as a writer has led to some misunderstanding as to the exact nature of the theory with which Brother Norton is unable to agree, for he appears to have entirely lost sight of it. It is not that " Dermott and his seventy or more associates of 1751 and 1752" were " Masonic saints of the highest standard," not even that Dermott himself was a Hebrew scholar and an educated gentleman, who never under any circumstances deviated from " the vantage ground of truth." I cannot therefore quite see how I have "totally failed" in doing that which I never attempted. I say that when elected Grand Secretary he was a journeyman painter, and I have plainly shown that those who aided him in forming a Grand Lodge were chiefly mechanics, shopkeepers, and labourers; but I must beg to differ most strongly with Brother Norton in his estimation of Dermott's character, especially when he would have us believe that he was a *forger*, as well as "the most shameless, impudent, and unscrupulous story-teller of all" Masonic historians or writers.

In order to prevent misconception in future, I will state as briefly as possible what my theory is, although I was certainly under the impression that I had already made it clear on pp. 4, 128 and 197 of the work under discussion. It will doubtless be sufficient if I state that one of the two Masonic bodies which in 1813 formed the United Grand Lodge of England has been credited by every one who has written on the subject since the year 1776 with having originally seceded from the other body (but the how, when and wherefore of this occurrence has hitherto been an open question), and that they have been invariably referred to as "*Seceders*," "*Schismatics*," or "*so-called Ancients.*" This, I say, is "the greatest fiction in the history of English Masonry."

My contention is that we have no right to apply these epithets to them, for there is not the shadow of a proof, nor has there ever been, that any considerable number of them at any time owned allegiance to the regular Grand Lodge of England established in 1717; that, in fact, they were Irish Masons, who in consequence of the doors of the English Lodges being closed against them had assembled in Lodges of their own formation, perfectly independent of any authority but that of their own selection until they felt themselves strong enough, and circumstances being favourable, to organize themselves into a Grand Lodge, which they did on the 27th Dec., 1753, having regularly assembled as a governing body under the denomination of a Grand Committee since the

I 1

17th July, 1751. Therefore, in my opinion, we are no
more justified in stigmatising them as "Seceders" or
"Schismatics" than we should be in applying these
epithets to certain tradesmen who, coming from a distant
town, set up in business in one where there was already
a firm carrying on a similar concern. This is my
principal argument. Now, with regard to the term
Antients, which former writers have applied in the
kind of left-handed way indicated, I look upon this as a
matter of merely secondary importance, and have so
treated it in my book.

What I say on this point, on page 196, in referring to
the Antients is, that "having kept alive and continued
to observe so many of the old customs of the Order
they had a stronger title to the appellation of Antients
than has been generally accorded them"; and on page
140 "I am inclined to think that undue importance is
attached to those designations, and that when the
Antients, or Irish Masons, first applied the term
Moderns to the adherents of the regular Grand Lodge
they were actuated more by a desire of making what
they doubtless considered a just and necessary distinction between the two societies than of using the
words in a derogatory sense. It was not till their prosperity and influence attracted notice, and the officials of
the rival community were called upon by their own
members to answer rather awkward questions, that the
bitterness of strife began, and the words 'Antient'
and 'Modern' became really important expressions." I
must take exception to one or two of Bro. Norton's
"Comments," which seem to me to require some
explanation. For instance, he says the first five or six
lodges of the Antients were dubbed "Time Imme-
morial." May I ask him who so described them? I
certainly did not; neither can I find that they themselves
claimed any such distinction. Again he says: "They
had no right to pretend to antiquity, or to the name of
Antients. With Bro. Norton's definition of what,
strictly speaking, *should be* "the line of demarcation

between *Ancient* and *Modern* Masons" I quite agree; but I think he will concede that Dermott and his associates had, at any rate, as good a title to call themselves "Antient Masons" as their rivals had to call themselves "Most Ancient," and as many other Masonic bodies of much more recent formation have to arrogate to themselves the name of *Ancient.* And as for their having "no right," &c., I fancy a good many of us do that which we have no *right* to do even in these enlightened days. For instance, Bro. Norton has no right to say: "Bro. Sadler, however, never saw a Warrant of the 'Ancients' older than 1772"; but he has said it nevertheless, and, more than that, he has printed it, an evident proof that he has not *carefully read* "Masonic Facts and Fictions," or he would have seen, on page 189, these words, "I have before me two original Warrants of the 'Ancients,' one granted in 1757, the other in 1759, and they contain no mention of *Prince Edwin*, nor even the 'Old Constitutions.'"

If my old friend will remind me when next we meet I shall have much pleasure in showing him these two documents. For the present, he must content himself with the transcript appended, and if he finds the word "York" in it I will readily forgive him.

BLESINTON GD. MASTER,
Wm. Holford D.G.M.

Jas. Nisbet S.G.W.   John Abercromby J.G.W

To ALL WHOM IT MAY CONCERN—

We the Grand Lodge in ample form assembled do hereby authorise and Impower our Trusty and well beloved Brethren, *Thomas Killingly,* MASTER, *James Wood,* SENR. WARDEN, and *William Baily,* JUNR. WARDEN (with their lawful assistants), To form and hold a Lodge of FREE AND ACCEPTED ANCIENT MASONS at the sign of the Punch Bowl, in Peck-Lane in the Town of Nottingham (or elsewhere) and in said Lodge Admit, Enter, and make Masons according to the Ancient and Honourable Custom of the Royal Craft in all Ages and Nations throughout the Known World.

No. LXII.

And we do hereby farther Impower our said Trusty and well-beloved Brethren Thomas Killingly, James Wood and William Baily (with their lawful Assistants) To Nominate Chuse and Instal their Successors, whom they are to invest with their power and Dignity, &c., and such Successors shall in like manner Nominate Chuse and Instal their Successors, &c., &c., &c., such Installations to be on every St. John's Day during the Continuance of this Lodge for Ever, providing the above Named Brethren and their Successors always pay due Respect to this Right Worshipful GRAND LODGE of Free and Accepted Ancient Masons, otherwise this Warrant to be of no force nor virtue.

Given under our hands and Seal of the Grand Lodge, London, this thirteenth day of April Anno Dom. 1757. Anno Lap. 5757.

LAU. DERMOTT, G.S.

The other Warrant, dated 6th day of June, 1759, is very similar to the older one, but it bears the additional words " Grand Lodge of York Masons, London (showing, as I have stated, that the adoption of the York tradition was an after-thought, and had nothing whatever to do with the origin of the Antients). Both of them bear what I believe to be the actual signature of Lord Blesinton, but what Bro. Norton would have us believe are merely forgeries of Dermott; they also bear the signatures of the D.G. Master and the Grand Wardens, and in my opinion one is as little likely to be a forgery as the others. Having carefully examined and compared these two signatures, I have no hesitation in saying that they were both written by the same person, and that person was *not* Laurence Dermott.

Although perfectly convinced myself of the genuineness of these documents, as well as of the authenticity of the correspondence relating to Lord Blesinton, alluded to by Bro. Norton in the *Chronicle*, No. 722, I felt that I ought to make an effort to satisfy the scruples of those who have not the opportunity of personally inspecting the original records. Accordingly, a few days ago I paid a visit to Sir Albert Woods (Garter King of Arms), our Grand Director of Ceremonies, to whom I am already under many obligations, and who is at all times most willing to assist me in my researches, both Masonic and otherwise. Sir Albert at once pointed out to me, in the official records, *three* different ways of spelling the title of the nobleman in question, viz., "Blesington," "Blessington," and "*Blesinton.*" He also informed me that the Will of the Countess of Blesinton was proved in the year 1774 (her husband died in 1769), and suggested that I should go to Somerset House, and ascertain how she spelt the name. He was also good enough to say that he would write to Ireland, and endeavour to obtain further information on the subject.

It really ought not to be necessary to remind a person of Bro. Norton's erudition that considerable license formerly existed in regard to the spelling of the family names of some of the nobility, and that what was generally deemed the most correct mode was the way the owner spelt it himself.

Bro. Norton in his "Comments" has given an example of this license in the name of "Heseltine," Dermott's formidable opponent,—which I find he persists in spelling *Hesseltine*, whereas I have adopted the same method as the owner. It would be almost as absurd on my part to suggest that Bro Norton purposely mis-spelt this name, in order to avoid an indictment for forgery, as it is for him to suggest that Dermott mis-spelt the name of Lord Blesinton for a similar reason.

I found, on examining the Will of the widow of Lord Blesinton, that she invariably signed it "E. Blesinton," and that wherever her late husband is mentioned in that document the name is spelt in the same way; this I take to be conclusive evidence that Dermott was not, in this instance at all events, a forger. If this is not sufficient to satisfy Bro. Norton, I have much pleasure in presenting him with *facsimiles* of the signatures of Lord Blesinton. The one of 1759 is copied from the Warrant of that date, and the other is copied from his lordship's Will, in Dublin.

Blesinton. 1759.

Blesinton. 1769.

I sincerely hope, for the credit of our Order, that we have now heard the last of this pitiful slander, which, originating in malicious rivalry more than a century ago, Bro. Norton has done his utmost to perpetuate, for want, I presume, of a more solid argument with which to support his peculiar views.

Bro. Norton seems to have taken an infinite deal of pains to prove that Laurence Dermott was a lying impostor and a forger, and that he and his associates " had no right to pretend to antiquity, or to the name of Ancients ; " indeed this is the substance of the whole of his " Comments." I cannot find one word either in support of the old " Secession fiction," or in opposition to my new theory of the "origin of the Antients;" hence I am placed in a somewhat difficult position, for I am at a loss to know whether he assents to that theory, or whether he rejects it. I am sure Bro. Norton will pardon me if I do not attempt to follow him through all the maze of figures, dates, and references by means of which he tries to fortify the position he has taken up as to the non-antiquity of the Antients, for, as previously remarked, I attach very little importance to the adoption of this title by the organizers of the Grand Lodge of 1753; they probably applied it in a different sense to what Bro. Norton does, and merely intended to imply that they practised the old customs, not those of the Modern Lodges. Indeed, I doubt very much whether they had any knowledge of the Ancient Masonry to which Bro. Norton refers. And so far from making myself responsible for all the sayings of Dermott to be found in my book, why I should just as readily undertake to be answerable for the assertions of Anderson, Preston, Oliver, and the rest of our historians ;—they all more or less drew upon their imagination when at a loss for direct evidence ;—and, moreover, I have distinctly expressed my doubts as to the correctness of some of his statements, and others I say are " scarcely worth a moment's consideration." Bro. Norton seems to forget that my non-secession theory is not based upon anything

said by Laurence Dermott, or any other individual, but
chiefly upon official documents now in existence, and
other evidence of a perfectly independent character,
quite unknown to former writers. In determining the
plan of "Masonic Facts and Fictions," I thought, whether
rightly or wrongly, that the best and fairest way would
be to examine, in the first instance, the records of the
older Grand Lodge, and extract every item of intelligence
that could possibly be construed into having any bearing
on the origin of the Antients. My next step was to
go through the same process with the records of the
opposition body, leaving my readers to draw their own
conclusions as to the existence of reliable evidence of
secession. In neither case could I find a particle of
evidence to justify any such conclusion; and if Bro.
Norton, or any one else can, I should be glad to have it
pointed out to me. There is, undoubtedly, plenty of
chaff, but very little wheat, and Bro. Norton appears to
have carefully selected the former, and utterly discarded
the latter. The *real* evidence on which my theory is
founded is contained in the last three chapters of the
book, and these he has not thought worthy of notice.

I will now endeavour to deal with some of Bro.
Norton's objections and assertions, in the order in which
they appear in his "Comments." First, as to the
adoption of the word "York." I say, in opposition to
an assertion of Preston's, that the Antients pretended
they were acting under the sanction of the Grand Lodge
at York, that they "never pretended that they were
acting under any such sanction" * * "What they
really did was this. They found Anderson's York tradition where it was of no particular use to any one"
(probably in the Irish book of Constitutions, for Dermott
took that book as the model of *his* first book of Constitutions); "and, with their usual foresight, they probably
conjectured that identifying *their* Institution with the
Grand Lodge, said to have been held at York in the
year 926, would give them an advantage over their
'Modern' rivals, especially amongst the Masons abroad;

they annexed the story accordingly, and embellished their Warrants with it." But this was an after-thought. Bro. Norton says, " It is evident, therefore, that before the revival of the York Grand Lodge he (Dermott) claimed authority from York." I want to know how it is evident, for at present I cannot see that adopting the name of " York Masons " is evidence of their having " claimed authority " from York? If it can be shown that application was made by the Antients to the Grand Lodge at York for authority or recognition, or even that they knew of the existence of a Grand Lodge at York, prior to 1761, other than the traditional one of A.D. 926, I am prepared to admit that there is something in Bro. Norton's assertion ; but bearing in mind how little was known in London of the real history of the old Lodge at York, even by the present generation of Masons, until they were enlightened by Bros. Hughan and Whytehead, it seems to me most unreasonable to conclude that Dermott had any knowledge of a Grand Lodge, or even a Lodge of any kind at York prior to its revival in 1761.

Bro. Norton ought to know that, figuratively speaking, York was as distant from London in 1756 as New York is at the present time, and as far as I can see, this old York Lodge was a " Grand Lodge " in name only, and if it had ever been known to the London Masons, it was probably forgotten before Dermott's time. Even Preston (and of course Bro. Norton will believe Preston) says the " York Constitution was entirely dropt in 1717." The most charitable view to take of his assertion is that the author of it believed he was correct, because he knew nothing to the contrary. I shall therefore, for the present at any rate, stick to my text, but if it be any satisfaction to Bro. Norton, I will readily admit that the Antients *had a pretence*, which was in posing as *English Masons* when, as a matter of fact, they were *Irish ;* but I think it not unlikely that when Dermott stated "there were numbers of old Masons then in (and adjacent to) London, from whom the present Grand Lodge of Ancient Masons received the old system, without adulteration," he was under the impression that certain alterations, which I am of opinion were made in 1730, were really made in 1717, and that it was from these ante-Grand Lodge Masons that the Masons in Ireland derived their knowledge.

I trust I shall be excused if I omit to notice in detail Bro. Norton's references to "Masters' Words, and Degrees, Spratt's Constitutions," &c., for however much they may be opposed to the statements of Laurence Dermott I am unable to see that they have any bearing on either my theory or my evidence; I must, nevertheless, take exception to some of his assertions and arguments. For instance, he says that " Dermott was initiated in Dublin in 1746 ;" I should like to know his authority for that statement. I have been under the impression that the brother in question was initiated in 1741, and it is best to be correct when we can. Again, I must beg to differ from my friendly critic in his assumption that in 1739 the Dublin Masons *must* have known if any material alteration had been made in the English working in or after 1730, subsequent, in fact, to Lord Kingston's connection with the Grand Lodge of England. Neither can I see that a Committee appointed by the Grand Lodge of Ireland in 1739, on Anderson's new Constitutions, must necessarily be cognisant of any difference, not appertaining to the Laws and Regulations, between the two systems. Indeed, I think it highly probable that some of the *English Lodges* at a distance from London were many years before they were made acquainted with alterations in the ceremonies at that early period. It appears to me that Bro. Norton hardly realizes the great difference, socially and masonically, between the years 1730 and 1888.

2.

22nd DECEMBER, 1888.

AS it has pleased Bro. Norton to devote so large a portion of his criticism of " Masonic Facts and Fictions " to the abusing of Laurence Dermott, I must claim the indulgence of my readers while I endeavour, as in duty bound, to remove some of the odium which, in my opinion, has been thus unwarrantably cast upon his memory. During his lifetime, I should say, he was about the best hated man in Masonry, by one side, but he lived to a good old age, nevertheless, and generally managed to hold his own, although his detractors were many and powerful. I am very glad to be able to say that a large and increasing number of brethren take quite a different view of his character to what Bro. Norton does; and those who would like to know what can be said in his favour I recommend to read " Notes on Laurence Dermott and his Work," by Witham Matthew Bywater, published in London in 1884.

The concluding paragraph of this little book so clearly indicates the author's opinion of Dermott, and so well expresses my own, that I am tempted to reproduce it here in the hope that it may serve to counteract the effect of some of the mud with which Bro. Norton has so liberally bespattered him. " The zeal and success with which he devoted a large portion of his life to the service of the Craft; the many battles which he fought against her enemies within and without; his staunch and inflexible adherence to the ancient landmarks of the Order, and the vast knowledge which he brought to bear upon his work, justly entitle him not only to the encomiums which his Grand Lodge pronounced upon him, but to the generous admiration of his brethren in succeeding ages."

Nothing would afford me greater pleasure than to discuss with Bro. Norton every one of his imaginary grievances against Dermott, and I make no doubt he will admit that the greater part of them *are* imaginary, after he has read these lines; but it is so much easier to cast aspersions than it is to disprove them. I must therefore content myself with adverting only to such as are easily refuted, but the reader will please *not* to infer that my omitting to notice others indicates acquiescence in them.

Bro. Norton's third grievance strikes me at first sight as being so peculiarly inconsistent that I really cannot pass it over without comment. " Third, the dubbing of his Constitutions 'Ahiman Rezon' was designed to impose on his dupes that he was a *Hebrew Scholar.* The said words, however, are not *Hebrew,* and were a pure invention of Dermott."

Now, if there were an atom of truth in this assertion Dermott *must* have been an out and out fool, but Bro. Norton himself admits that he was a " clever and well-informed man." How any *sane* man could expect to gain credit for being a "Hebrew scholar" by making use of words which "are *not* Hebrew" is a mystery beyond my powers to solve. I give it up. It appears to me that his dupes (?) must have " multiplied and increased exceedingly," for the book went through eight editions in England, and the title was readily adopted by the Grand Lodge of Ireland, and many of the American Grand Lodges ; but what I want to know is, where is the evidence of the design to impose? Can Bro. Norton refer me to anything said or written by Dermott which could possibly be construed into a desire that the words " Ahiman Rezon " should be accepted as Hebrew? If he cannot, he has no right to make such an assertion ; but if he can, I apologise to him at once. That Dermott knew something of the Hebrew characters is evident, from his having used them in writing his own name at the end of his first Minute Book; but the extent of his knowledge in this direction I will not attempt to surmise. I must, however, confess that at present I am ignorant of any indication that he wished to be considered a Hebrew scholar ; and as for the words being " a pure invention of Dermott," which I must beg leave to doubt, I fail to see any crime in a man inventing a title for his own book.

On the supposition that Dermott considered the Masons of Scotland, Ireland, and many parts of America, together with those of his own jurisdiction in England, as Antient Masons, I see nothing extraordinary or inconsistent in his saying, " The number of Antient

Masons, compared with the Moderns, being as ninety-nine to one, proves the universality of the old Order, &c., &c."

In a foot-note on page 243 of the *Chronicle*, Bro. Norton has referred to a certain prayer which Dr. Oliver says was the joint composition of Anderson and Manningham, in or about 1754. I assume that my exposure of this fiction on page 9 of " Masonic Facts and Fictions" has escaped Bro. Norton's notice, or he would have mentioned it ; but if he turns to the page named he may read as follows :—" Now, as Dr. Anderson died, and I presume was decently buried in 1739, and whereas Manningham did not appear on the Masonic stage until 1747, and was not appointed Deputy Grand Master till 1752, how these two worthy doctors could have held a consultation passes my comprehension." I fear Bro. Norton will think me very hard to please, and I really am very sorry for being so troublesome, but I must call his attention to a little mistake, quite unintentional I know, in the first paragraph of his second article, wherein he refers in the following words to my reasons for imagining that alterations were made in the ceremonies in the year 1730: " And this theory he derived, not from the records, but from something he read here and something there, which, with the aid of a little imagination, he persuaded himself that the Grand Lodge of England authorised, as innovations, in 1730."

It is true I have not much to complain of here. I would merely ask what is Bro. Norton's definition of the term " records," if the written minutes of the Grand Lodge, the written minutes of the Lodge of Promulgation, and original letters to the Grand Secretary do not come under that definition ?

These are my chief sources of information, which can easily be verified by a reference to pp. 39, 40, 145, 153, 156, 157 and 162 of " Masonic Facts and Fictions." On page 39 I give several extracts from the Grand Lodge Minutes, the first of which must suffice for my present purpose. On the 28th August, 1730, "Dr. Desaguliers stood up, and (taking Notice of a printed Paper lately published and dispersed about the Town, and since inserted in the Newspapers, Pretending to discover and reveal the Misteries of the Craft of Masonry) recommended several things to the consideration of the Grand Lodge. Particularly the *Resolution of the last Quarterly Communication for preventing any false Brethren being admitted into Regular Lodges,* and such as call themselves Honorary Masons." "The Deputy Grand Master seconded the Doctor, and proposed several Rules to the Grand Lodge to be observed in their respective Lodges, for their security against all open and secret enemies of the Craft."

It will be observed that in the preceding extract reference is made to a " Resolution of the last Quarterly Communication for preventing false Brethren," &c., &c. As a matter of fact, no such Resolution appears, either in the minutes of the "last Quarterly Communication," or of any previous meeting, and the only way I can account for the omission is that the said Resolution, and also the *several things recommended* "to the consideration of the Grand Lodge " had some relation to the ceremonies, and were not considered proper to be written, or why the omission ? I should very much like to hear Bro. Norton's explanation of this matter. Surely he would not wish us to believe that he is so utterly ignorant of the traditions and established customs of the Grand Lodge of England as not to be aware that nothing of an esoteric character was, or is, ever recorded in the minutes of the Grand Lodge.

At the following meeting of the Grand Lodge, *i.e.*, on the 15th December, 1730, "the Deputy Grand Master took notice of a pamphlet, lately published by one Pritchard, who pretends to have been made a regular Mason, &c., &c.," and a resolution was passed relating to the admission of visitors. With reference to this incident, I say, on page 40, " assuming that both these extracts refer to one pamphlet, it appears as though something unusual had occurred between the 28th August and the 15th December, or the second and more emphatic notice would not have been either judicious or necessary . . . . Pritchard is said to have made an affidavit before an alderman on the 13th of October, that his publication was a " true copy of Freemasonry." It seems to me most unlikely that he should have taken this extraordinary step unless under the fear that his book was in danger of being discredited in consequence of some important alteration having taken place in the recognized ceremonies." I would also direct Bro. Norton's attention to page 156, where he may read, " I have already noticed the sensation created by the publication of Pritchard's pamphlet in 1730, when the D.G M. recommended several things to the consideration of the Grand Lodge ; " and I will now state, without fear of contradiction, that in no part of the records is there a passage so capable of being interpreted as forming a prelude to an alteration in the recognized forms as the one referred to.

A second edition of a rather curious, and now scarce book on Masonry, was published in London in 1766, which professes to show the difference between the Antient and Modern systems. The writer states that the E.A.'s word was formerly the F.C.'s, till a pretended discovery of Freemasonry came out, wrote by Samuel Pritchard, and still continues to be published to this time. . . . . But in order to prevent being imposed upon by cowans or impostors, who might want to gain admittance, from his performance, the Fraternity held a General Council, and the E.A.'s and F.C.'s words were reversed, and Private Accounts transmitted to each Lodge, though there are some unconstituted Lodges who still retain the former Custom." I am unable to give the period of the first edition of this book, but it was probably some years earlier, leaving an interval of about 30 years only from the first appearance of Pritchard's pamphlet, it is therefore easy to conceive that the writer had good grounds for his statement.

On page 145 appears " The following extract, from an original letter dated 15th October 1776," which seems to have been written at the instigation of the Duke of Athole, Grand Master of the Antients, by a Captain Geo. Smith, himself a Modern. I need only give two of the four questions in the book which " His Grace, &c., would wish to know."

" 2. Why the G.L. of England has thought propper to alter the mode of Initiation ; also the Word, Pas-word and Grip of the different Degrees in Masonry."

" 3. Whether Dermot constitutes Lodges in his own Name or in the name and Authority of the Duke of Athol, and whether anything can be laid to his charge inconsistent with the character of an honest man and a Mason." I cannot find the reply to this letter.

The following is a portion of a letter from Major Shirreff (an Antient), dated 27th June, 1785, and in order to save Bro. Norton the trouble of searching for it I may mention that it is to be found on page 153. " I was Introduced into this Noble Institution according to the most Antient manner, and that you may understand me more clearly, when a Candidate is presented to me, my first instruction to him springs from the Second Le'r of the Alphabet, and I never knew but one Lodge since I have been a Bro'r that ever began with the ninth Le'r, I have met with several Brothers that have been Initiated so, but all such I was from the first told were call'd Modern Masons." These letters were addressed to the Grand Secretary of the Moderns, and, in all probability, have never been read since they were endorsed and put away, until I turned them out in searching for materials for " Masonic Facts and Fictions." However, should any one feel so disposed, he is at liberty to satisfy himself that they are genuine documents and are not manipulated for my own purposes.

I will now ask Bro. Norton to read the following extracts (he will find them on pp. 161 and 162), from the minutes of the Lodge of Promulgation, to the proceedings of which he appears to attach so little importance,

K

although I cannot help remarking that in his "Comments" he has been exceedingly careful in avoiding whatever portions of them appear to support my views: however, I freely forgive him, for I honestly believe he has done his best. "At the next meeting, on the 28th Dec. eighteen members of the Lodge and forty Masters of other Lodges attended, and the 'R.W.M. took a retrospective view of the proceedings of the Lodge of Promulgation.' I need not reproduce everything that was said and done on this occasion; no doubt the following extract will be sufficient for our present purpose :—' The R.W.M. therefore proceeded to point out the material parts in and between the several Degrees to which the attention of the Masters of Lodges would be requisite in preserving the Ancient Landmarks of the Order—such as the form of the Lodge, the number and situation of the Officers—their different distinctions in the different Degrees—the restoration of the proper words to each Degree, and the making of the Pass words *between* one Degree and another, instead of *in* the Degree." Knowing how sceptical Bro. Norton sometimes is as to the reliability of printed history, and justly so, I will here remind him that I quote from the original minutes, and that the words in italics are so distinguished in the minute book.

Although Bro. Norton and I differ materially in our interpretation of the word "Ancient," and I fear we must agree to differ, there ought to be no difference between us as to the meaning of the word "records," he will, therefore, I make no doubt, on reconsideration, readily admit that he is mistaken in saying that my theory is *not* derived from the records; and as for the "something he read here and something there," I would remind him that it is by careful research and the simple process of putting "this and that together" that I have been able to deduce conclusions which although not acceptable to him are perfectly clear and satisfactory to some hundreds of other readers. If Bro. Norton *will* prefer the unsupported and partial assertions of Preston I cannot

help it, but I think, in common fairness, he ought to
show some reliable grounds for his preference ; I readily
admit the truth of his somewhat sarcastic remark, that
my "*veneration* does not extend to Preston," and I think
I have already given several good and tangible reasons
for my disbelief in him, one of which would satisfy most
thoughtful persons, *i.e.*, that he was a malicious and
partizan writer. I was certainly under the impression
that I had dealt very leniently with him in my book, only
saying enough, indeed, to show that he was not a
reliable historian, and this, it appears, has entirely
escaped the notice of Bro. Norton, for he makes no
allusion to it. As a matter of principle I prefer to—

"Let the dead Past bury its dead."

but since he makes such wonderment of my want of
veneration for Preston, I feel constrained to present
him with a brief sketch of the Masonic career of that
Brother, from *my* point of view, and in so doing I shall
refrain from imputing motives, but confine myself to
historical facts gleaned from his biography and Grand
Lodge records.

William Preston was initiated in a Lodge under
the sanction of the Antients. In less than two years
he deserted that body and went over to the enemy,
taking his Lodge, or as many of its members as
he could with him. In the rival society he soon came
to the front, and tried his utmost, by misrepresentation, to annihilate the body that had first received him
into Masonry. Having entered the service of the Grand
Lodge, he obtained access to the records, and was
thereby enabled to write what he called a History of
Masonry, which was printed in the Freemasons' Calendar.
He obtained the sanction of the Grand Master for pub-
lishing his " Illustrations of Masonry," and the book was
extensively advertised in the Grand Lodge Circular,
along with the Book of Constitutions. After a while, he
and a few others rebelled against the constituted
authorities, and were very properly expelled ; where-
upon they started a schismatic society, and called it a

K I

"Grand Lodge," which ignominiously failed, after a precarious existence of about ten years. They then apologised for their misconduct, and petitioned to be restored to their Masonic privileges; and their petition was eventually granted. We do not find his name amongst those of the worthy Brethren who worked long and patiently to heal the differences between the two rival societies in England, and who ultimately succeeded in completing what has been aptly described as the "Glorious Union of 1813," but we *do* know that in 1812 he issued another edition of his book, which, together with the mendacious statements concerning the Antients, previously formulated, contained fresh matter of an irritating nature—or, at all events, such as would not be likely to assist in consummating the desires of the leading members of the two Fraternities. There can be no doubt that Preston possessed abilities of no mean order, and, in my opinion, had he devoted them to this laudable object, the Union might have been brought about some years earlier than it was. However, this is a mere matter of opinion. But to return to historical facts. Shortly after the former rival bodies had, in the face of enormous difficulties, which "can better be imagined than described"—after several years of patient labour—agreed upon a system of ceremonies and lectures which were to be recognised as orthodox for the future, and which had only been arrived at by mutual conciliation. Preston died, and it was found that he had left two legacies to the Grand Lodge, one of £500 to the Fund of Benevolence, and the other, the interest of £300, for the annual delivery of *his* lecture.

Of the first of these legacies I cannot speak too highly; but, as for the second, it appears to me that if he had wished to promote and *perpetuate discord*, he could not have done anything more likely to produce that result. I must confess that *I fail* to see anything in the character, thus depicted, to inspire *veneration*. If Bro. Norton is more successful, he is heartily welcome, so far as I am concerned, to *venerate* as much as he pleases. I make

him a present of his *idol*, together with his legacies, his
History of Masonry, and his Prestonian Lecture into the
bargain.

Laurence Dermott is quite good enough for me : the
man who stuck to *his colours* from first to last, and stood
his ground in the face of tremendous odds ; who inspired
his raw recruits with his own indomitable pluck ; and
although he did not live long enough to lead them to
victory, he taught them how to gain it, and fell fighting ;
the man who lived down slander and misrepresentation,
alike discreditable to the originators and to those who
persist in perpetuating them ; who expressed a hope
that he would " live to see a general conformity and
unity between the worthy Masons of all denominations ;"
and who, although comparatively a poor man, gave up
the profits of the fourth and all future editions of his
book for the relief of the poor and needy of the Craft he
loved, and had so long and faithfully served.

3.

29th DECEMBER, 1888.

IT would be extremely gratifying to me if I could but
find in Bro. Norton's " Comments " something that
would enable us to meet on level ground, as it were, and
enjoy a real brotherly " shake " of sympathy and cordial
agreement ; and, indeed, I was under the impression
that I had reached that delightful stage when I read, in
his first article, that the Irish Grand Lodge derived all
its ceremonies from the London Grand Lodge; but
when, in his second article, he tells us that " the installation of Masters, with words, signs and grips thereunto
belonging, was an early Irish *invention*, and so were the
Officers known as ' Senior and Junior Deacons,'" I find
we are nearly as far apart as ever ; and yet it is only
the one little word " invention " that separates us. I
am curious to know what authority other than Bro.
Norton's imagination there is for saying that the ceremony referred to was an *Irish invention* ; if he turns to

pages 34 and 196 of that troublesome book of mine he will find that allusion is made to a Postscript to the *Constitutions* of 1723, and if he compares that Postscript with " The antient manner of constituting a Lodge " in Spratt's Irish Constitutions, I think he will admit that there exists a strong family likeness ; and if he makes a comparison between " Spratt," Anderson's edition of 1738, and Dermott's "Ahiman Rezon," he will find a still closer resemblance.   In each of the books named the ceremony of installation is described quite as clearly as I should expect to find it in an authorised publication, and unless Bro. Norton can produce *evidence* that this ceremony was practised in Ireland prior to 1723 I shall prefer to believe that it was *not* an " Irish invention," but that it was taken from England originally, and was afterwards restored by the Irish Masons, or Antients, when the English Fraternity had neglected to practice it for so long a period that it was quite unknown to the general body of the Craft.

I am sorry to say I cannot accept the assertion that the Moderns never had a ceremony of installation, for it appears to me to be of a similar character to many other of Bro. Norton's assertions, *i.e.,* it is contrary to evidence.   In order to enable those who have not access to the books just mentioned to judge for themselves, I will quote a paragraph from the Postscript to the Constitutions of 1723 :—

" Upon this the *Deputy* shall rehearse the *Charges* of a *Master*, and the GRAND MASTER shall ask the *candidate*, saying, *Do you submit to these* Charges, as MASTERS have *done* in all Ages?   And the candidate signifying his cordial submission thereunto, the GRAND MASTER shall, by CERTAIN significant ceremonies and ancient usages, install him, and present him with the *Constitutions*, the Lodge Book, and the *instruments* of his office, not altogether, but one after another ; and after each of them, the *Grand Master*, or his *Deputy*, shall rehearse the short and pithy *Charge* that is suitable to the thing presented."   I am quite unaware of the extent of Bro.

Norton's knowledge of the English ceremony of installation, for I have no recollection of the subject ever having been mentioned, either in our correspondence or on the occasions of our meeting; but having myself had some years of practice, I may observe that this quotation seems to bear a very striking resemblance to a portion of the authorised ceremony of the present day.

If I am not mistaken, there is in Boston an excellent Masonic Library, to which Bro. Norton is at all times welcome, and, although I know him to be a very busy man, yet I think it will be worth his while when he *can* spare a few hours to carefully read the whole of this Postscript, and also the descriptions in the Constitutions of the Annual Grand Feasts. Prior to 1717 he will find a long list of persons of one sort or another who are said to have been Grand Masters. This Bro. Norton knows as well as I do, but he may not have remarked that none of these personages are represented to have been installed; indeed, the word is not used at all, so far as I can see. At the Feast in 1717, and for several years afterwards, the Grand Master, if present at the Annual Feast, is said to have been "installed." According to the written minutes of Grand Lodge, the last Grand Master of that period to whom this term is applied is Viscount Montague, who was installed on the 18th April, 1732; from thence till 1782 the word is only used once, and that is in 1764, when John Revis was installed as proxy for Lord Blayney. And in 1782 the Earl of Effingham went through a similar process for the Duke of Cumberland.

Here, then, in my opinion, is fairly conclusive evidence that in the early days of the Grand Lodge the Moderns had a ceremony of installation for private Lodges as well as for the Grand Lodge; but why they were discontinued I can only surmise. In the latter case it could not have been out of consideration for the appetites of the brethren, as the ceremony always took place *after dinner*. A possible clue may be found in the following incidents:—

In 1730 the Duke of Norfolk is not stated to have been installed, but only "declared" Grand Master; his predecessors had all been installed, and in 1731 Lord Lovell, his successor, was "so very ill of an Ague that he was obliged to return home, but that he had appointed the Right Hon. the Lord Coleraine to be his Proxy for that day." After dinner Lord Coleraine was accordingly *invested* with the Badge of Grand Master as Proxy for Lord Lovell. It may be that finding that these two got on very well without a formal ceremony of installation the brethren did not attach any importance to that function, for although the next Grand Master, Lord Montague, is said to have been "install'd," his immediate successors are all described as having merely been "invested," or "declared." Private Lodges would probably follow the Grand Lodge in this respect, and in course of time the ceremony of installation was no longer deemed a part of the modern system of Free-masonry.

As for my trying to prove "that the Antients' form of Installation was truly *ancient*, or even as old as 1723," I am not likely to attempt anything of the kind, for it certainly is not possible to do so, neither do I consider it necessary. It is quite sufficient for my purpose if I prove that the Moderns had *no* ceremony of Installation when the Antients or Irish Masons started their Grand Lodge, and the latter had, thus showing that their customs were different, and the inconsistency of the secession theory; and this is also my reason for quoting the minutes of the Lodge of Promulgation with reference to Deacons, which Bro. Norton says "were not an ancient landmark." But as I never said they were, this piece of information seems quite superfluous.

I find I must take exception to another assertion about that terrible fellow Dermott, and, as in the former case, I find we are very nearly agreed until Bro. Norton allows his imagination to get the better of his judgment and common sense. On page 259 of the *Chronicle* he says:— "Hence he was persuaded that the Irish ritual was ancient, or more in accordance with the old ritual of Solomon, or at least of the one used at York in the days of Prince Edwin, and he therefore may have felt himself justified in doing what he did. But, although he must afterwards have been better informed, he still continued to swear, through thick and thin, that his Grand Lodge was ancient, and the old one modern." I should like to know the authority for "must afterwards have been better informed," and also for the swearing business. So far as I know Dermott never did anything of the kind. The purport of his claim was that the *ceremonies* and *customs* of the body to which he belonged were *ancient*, but I am not aware that he ever pretended his Grand Lodge was older than 1753.

Now, with regard to the Resolution passed in Grand Lodge on 12th April, 1809, at the recommendation of the Committee of Charity, consisting of all Grand Officers, Past Grand Officers, and Masters of Lodges in good standing, Bro. Norton says in effect that he does not believe this body of Masons knew what they were talking about, consequently the Grand Lodge that adopted their recommendation must have been in a similar state of darkness. It is somewhat difficult to make out from these " Comments " what Bro. Norton *does* believe, and I occasionally find myself wondering whether he *believes anything* beyond the range of his own eyesight. but with all due respect to *him*, I must say that it appears to me that the brethren of 1809 *ought* to have been better acquainted with the subject of their " motion " than Bro. Norton is to-day ; he will, there-fore, I trust, permit me to stick to my text, *i.e.*, that they knew " they had previously departed from the *Ancient Landmarks* of the order, and were ignorant of the precise period when this event occurred." As for their not knowing what the " Ancient Landmarks " were, probably they did not, according to Bro. Norton's definition, for this is a phrase even more elastic than the word " ancient "; but they evidently knew enough for their own purposes, for the said " motion " was passed in a very numerously attended Grand Lodge without a division.

I shall not reply at length to Bro. Norton's "Comments" on my simple statement as to the non-observance, by the Moderns, of the popular Saints' days; but as he has given me credit for a much more powerful imagination than I can fairly lay claim to, I think it better to repeat what I *did* say than to attempt to defend what I did not.

"I shall now endeavour to show, that apart from the question of form or ceremony, innovations upon the ancient usages and established customs of the Order had, at different times, been countenanced by the leaders of the regular Grand Lodge ; that from the advent of the aristocratic element in such large numbers, the Society had undergone a process of what, for want of a better word, I shall call modernizing. The 24th June and the 27th of December were literally ' *red letter days* ' in the old Masonic Calendar, and are still regarded by many of the Fraternity with veneration " . . . .

" Indeed, the Saints John days were generally looked upon as *the* days for all-important Masonic gatherings, not only in this country, but in Scotland and Ireland also. Our first Grand Master (Anthony Sayer) was elected and installed on St. John Baptist's day, 1717, and this day was adhered to by the Grand Lodge for the installation of his successors until 1725, when, "being unprovided with a new noble Grand Master, the officers were continued six months longer." Lord Paisley was, however, installed on the 27th December following ; Lord Inchiquin on the 27th February, 1727 ; Lord Coleraine on the 27th December of the same year ; and Lord Kingston on the 27th December, 1728. From this time forward the "regulars" seem to have been utterly oblivious to the fact,—

That saints will aid if men will call,

for the eighteen installations between 1730 and 1753 appear to have taken place on a day best suited to the convenience of the noble personages most concerned,

and not once on either of the popular Saints' days.
Now this irreverent disregard of an old custom was not
likely to strengthen their claims to antiquity when put
forth at a later period."

" The Antients from the first seem to have been
most scrupulous in selecting one or the other of these
days for their Grand ceremonials."

I give this as one of several instances of neglect on
the part of the regular Grand Lodge of the old customs
whereby they had earned for themselves the appellation
of Moderns, it is a simple statement of facts, and
my explanation of it happens to be the true one; it was
done to suit the convenience of the different noble
Grand Masters, for the day of the Grand Feast was
invariably left to their selection, as the minutes of
Grand Lodge show, and as Bro. Jacob Norton might
have seen had he read the paragraph of Anderson's
immediately following the one he quotes :—

" But of late years most of the *Eminent* Brethren
being out of town on both the St. John's Days, the
Grand Master has appointed the *Feast* on such a
Day as appeared most convenient to the *Fraternity*.
This is what Dr. Anderson said in 1738, and no doubt
it was the real reason, if we read the concluding
words thus ; *to himself and his successor*, instead of "to
the *Fraternity*." Bro. Norton's method of dealing with
this portion of " Facts and Fictions " is. to say the
least of it, most peculiar. I can only afford space for
a sample of it.

" Again, the Ancients observed St. John's Day, but
the Moderns ceased to observe it after 1730 ; hence our
worthy brother imagines that the Moderns were guilty
of removing an ancient landmark. The truth, however,
is the observance of Saint John's Day is not an ancient
landmark at all, &c. Now, as I did not mention the
word " landmark " in this connection, and certainly
never attempted to define it in any part of the book, it
seems to me that my old friend has taken an infinite
deal of unnecessary trouble to demolish a "guy," created

entirely out of his *own imagination*, for in order to obtain
the requisite materials he appears to have hunted far and
near, and to have mixed up Jews, Christians, Roman
Catholics and Reformation, Saints and sinners, Dr.
Anderson and the Virgin Mary, with the misdeeds of
American Masonic luminaries, into a mass which defies
all my efforts to penetrate. I imagine, however, from
the purport of his concluding remarks that this saintly
subject must be rather a sore point with him, and on the
principle that any peg is good enough to hang a
complaint on he availed himself of the opportunity
I had given him to retaliate for some grievance he has
against our brethren over the water.

I cannot agree with Bro. Norton as to the possibility
of Israelitish objections having had anything to do with
the non-observance of the Saints' days by the Grand
Lodge, for although our registers show that in the latter
half of the last century a large number of that sect
entered the Order, it is difficult to ascertain to which
branch they gave the preference. I am, however, inclined
to the opinion that, at the Union in 1813, the Antients
had the larger number of Jews on their register. I have
not thought it necessary to go thoroughly into this
matter, but I may mention two Lodges that were certainly
founded by brethren of the Jewish faith, viz., the Lodge
of Israel, No. 205, constituted by the Antients in 1793,
and the Hiram's Lodge, constituted by the Moderns
in 1781.

Bro. Norton's mother Lodge (Joppa, No. 188) seems
to have been a mixed Lodge from the first, but judging
from the names on the register in 1813, I should say it
was then composed chiefly, if not entirely, of Jewish
brethren ; it may interest him to know that about the
year 1758 the person with whom he is so exceedingly
angry—the much-abused Dermott—had sufficient good
sense to slightly alter the wording of his Warrants,
which, I have no doubt, was done in order to meet the
views of Israelitish brethren : for, instead of stating that
" Installations are to be on every St. John's Day," as at

first, subsequent Warrants read "on (or near) every St. John's Day." My answer to the assertion "Even the Ancients never found fault with their opponents for not keeping Saints' Days," is the following extract from a resolution unanimously passed in their Grand Lodge on the 6th June, 1810, having reference to the terms on which they were prepared to consider the question of an union of the two societies : " and that the Grand Lodge shall be convened and held quarterly, on a given day in each quarter, for communication with the Craft, besides the anniversary meetings of St. John the Evangelist and St. John the Baptist."

4.

5th JANUARY, 1889.

MUST beg to be excused entering into a discussion as to the truth or falsity of Dermott's account of Sir Christopher Wren's Grand Mastership ; possibly Bro. Norton may be right ; if so Dermott, of course, must have been wrong, as many other historians have been who have had better opportunities for ascertaining the truth than a journeyman painter could have had in the middle of the last century. For my own part, I am not disposed to accept either Anderson's or Dermott's account of the origin and formation of the Grand Lodge of 1717 as perfectly reliable ; and, moreover, I do not expect to find any man infallible, not even Bro. Norton, who, in my opinion, is unjust to himself in stating that he disbelieves "anything and everything that was written by Dermott, and even his Grand Lodge records are, in my opinion, utterly unworthy of credence." I am not quite sure that we agree as to what should come under the definition of "records," but I think the term ought certainly to include the Minute Books and Registers of the Grand Lodge ; if these are what Bro. Norton deems "unworthy of credence" I am fairly puzzled to know what, in his opinion, *is* worthy of credence. I know he has seen some of the Registers, but am not sure that he has examined the Minute Books. If he has not, his expression of opinion ought not to influence any one, and if he has, I am quite certain it will not affect the views of those brethren who are personally familiar with them, and are quite as capable of forming an opinion as to their credibility as he is. I always like to give honour where honour is due, and shall, therefore, without hesitation, assign to Bro. Jacob Norton the merit of having been the very first to give expression to an opinion that the Grand Lodge records of the Antients are " unworthy of credence."

It is just possible, however, that there *may* be some few inquisitive people scattered about the world who would like to know something more about the said " records " before coming to a conclusion. It is but fair, therefore, that I should state that they are not *printed books*, but the veritable written transactions of the various meetings, in the handwriting of the different Grand Secretaries, recorded at the time of occurrence—those written by Dermott himself, which I assume that Bro. Norton considers as *most* "unworthy of credence," embracing a period when, in their wildest dreams of future power and prosperity the Antients could never have imagined such an event would ever come to pass as an union on more than equitable terms with their formidable opponents, who affected to hold them in so much contempt. These books were handed over, with the other property of the Antients, to the custody of the officials of the United Grand Lodge some twenty-four years after the death of Dermott; and I can safely say that they have never been tampered with from the time they were written to the present day.

With regard to the incident which first raised Bro. Norton's suspicions of Dermott's natural propensity for forging documents ; we all know how easy it is to discover faults if we set out in search of them, and this. it appears, is what Bro. Norton has done all through his investigation of this question of the Antients. Hence his frequent mistakes. I will readily admit that he is very much at a disadvantage in the matter of obtaining information, whereas I have every facility of daily and hourly access to original records and documents such as no other person has ever had, or, at all events, no one of this generation has ever availed himself of. The great difference between us may be accounted for by the fact that in approaching an historical subject I do so with strict impartiality. I look for *truth* and reliable evidence, and have met with a fair amount of success; hence I can see nothing inconsistent or extraordinary in the incident which first awakened Bro. Norton's suspicions, of course bearing in mind the great difference between the years 1757 and 1888, and the *fact* that the second letter, which he refers to as having been read in the Grand Lodge in 1762 was not read until exactly *ten years after that date*, viz., on the 2nd September, 1772.

In dealing with this very difficult subject, it must be admitted that Bro. Gould has treated it most carefully and most exhaustively, according to the information at his command; and if Bro. Norton will again refer to page 446 of the second volume of his very valuable work he will, I make no doubt, readily admit that *he* has made the mistake and not Bro. Gould. That a Deputy Grand Secretary in 1772 should not be well posted in everything that was said and done by a Grand Secretary in the name of his Grand Lodge fifteen years previously is not a matter of surprise to me. In all probability he was not even a Mason in 1757, and was not appointed to the office of D.G.S. until 1768. Bro. Calder, who held the office of Grand Secretary of Ireland in 1757, was superseded in 1767 for negligence, and so far as I can learn he had no connection with the Grand Lodge in 1772. The very fact of this and other correspondence being mentioned in the Transactions is, in my opinion, strong presumptive evidence, not of Dermott's duplicity, but of his honesty. The letter of 1772 is apparently copied *verbatim* into the minute book; and I am almost certain that if Bro. Norton were to read it the recollection

of his having expressed an opinion that it was forged or
concocted by Dermott would bring a blush of shame to
his good-natured and expressive countenance. Dermott
was undoubtedly by far the best and most painstaking
Grand Secretary the Antients ever had—hence his
practice of recording apparently trivial matters, which a
less scrupulous person would have omitted.

Having, I think, in previous articles, conclusively
disposed of the assertion that "all the Warrants given
by the Antients during the Grand Mastership of the
Earl of Blessington have somehow disappeared," I need
not dilate at any great length on the statement as
to there being a Warrant as well as a Deputation in
Nova Scotia, which although headed *Blesinton* are
not signed by the Grand Master, but by " Lau. Dermott,
G. Sec."   At present I have only Bro. Norton's unsup-
ported assertion on the one side ; and, on the other, the
Transactions of " Grand Lodge at the Five Bells Tavern,
7th Dec^r., 1757," one of the items reading thus :—
" Heard petitions from His Excellency Charles Lawrence
Governor of Nova Scotia, Major Erasmus James Philips,
Esq., William Nisbett, Esq., Alexander Murray, Esq., and
57 others praying to be warranted, viz., one Provincial
Grand Warrant and two private Warrants for the
Province of Nova Scotia."   "Order'd that the Grand
Secretary shall immediately prepare the said Warrants,
&c."   Now, to my thinking, this business seems all fair
and above board ; and unless Bro. Norton can produce
reliable evidence to the contrary, I shall prefer to believe
that there was as little forgery in this as in the case of
Warrants issued in England.

To Bro. Norton's next question, "What kind of a
Grand Master did Lord Blessington make ? "   I answer,
unhesitatingly, as good an one as any other of that
period, and better than many on either side, notwith-
standing that he did not attend a single meeting of the
Grand Lodge, " and was installed in his own library in
Margaret Street."   The correspondence relating to Lord
Blesinton's first election as Grand Master of the

Antients is given *in extenso* on pp. 84, 85, 86 of "Masonic Facts and Fictions," and it will be observed that his Lordship says, "As I shall be out of Town St. John's Day, I must beg leave to act by Deputy." This letter was read in Grand Lodge on the 27th December (St. John's Day), 1756, and afterwards "the Grand Lodge proceeded to the Instalment of Grand Master, which was done by proxy in the person of the Honourable Edward Vaughan, Esq., who Rec'd all the Honours, &c., &c., &c." And then the Grand Secretary proclaimed the new Grand Master, so that, as a matter of fact, he was installed in the same way as several of the Grand Masters on the Modern side. I find, on referring to the Grand Lodge minutes that Bro. Norton is mistaken in saying that " the evidence of Lord Blessington's private installation rests solely on Dermott's testimony," for the statement in question was *not made* by Dermott, but by the Deputy Grand Master (William Dickey), at a meeting of the Grand Lodge on the 25th November, 1767, in the presence of the Grand Master and several other distinguished Masons, as well as the members of the Grand Lodge.

It appears that a Bro. Thomas Forsyth had a grievance, and nothing would satisfy him but to air it in Grand Lodge; the complaint from which he suffered was caused by his having been left out in the cold when the Grand Master (the Hon. Thomas Mathew) was installed privately in 1767. In his own words " he did deem the Grand Master smuggled into the Grand Lodge, by which means the D.G.M. and the rest of the Grand Officers had absolutely trampled upon the good laws of Masons, &c." To which the D.G.M. replied, " That the Transaction complained of was not contrary to custom nor General Regulations. That Grand Masters in England and *Ireland* have been (at their own request) Installed in private. and that such Installations were never disputed, particularly the late Grand Master Earl of Blesinton, who was privately Install'd by the G^d Officers & Secretary in his Lordship's *Liberary* in Margret Street."

L

" The Grand Master arose and acquainted the Brethren that he stood up to confirm what the Deputy had said. That he was privately Install'd by the Grand Officers and Secretary ; that being Unanimously chosen he did not see where the objection could be made, &c." I should rather like to give the whole of the minutes of this meeting, for they are amusing as well as interesting; but as Bro. Norton thinks the records of the Antients " utterly unworthy of credence," it would be useless to do so. I may, however, remark that this statement was made during the lifetime of Lord Blesinton, and it has never been disputed before that I am aware of.

Hitherto I have restricted myself to the very agreeable task of disproving Bro. Norton's assertions and upsetting his conclusions. I will now venture to express an opinion on my own account, which is :—That it is utterly impossible to arrive at a just appreciation of the value and authenticity of these old records without a minute examination of the originals, and that any expression of opinion as to their credibility, which is based on abbreviated extracts, is not worth the paper it is printed on. I find I must take exception to the assertion that since the Grand Mastership of the Duke of Montague the regular Grand Lodge of England had no great difficulty in finding a nobleman who would cheerfully accept the Grand Master's office. Bro. Norton says this " is an undoubted *fact;*" I say it is an undoubted *fiction.* In my last article I quote from the Grand Lodge minutes that the Installation in 1725 was postponed for six months because they were "unprovided with a new noble Grand Master," and several other instances of a similar character are on record ; indeed, this was the real origin of the abrogation of the Saints' Days for the Installation of Grand Master; it was also the reason of the departure from the old custom of having a new Grand Master every year.

It "*is* an undoubted *fact*" that they were " unprovided with a new noble Grand Master" in 1743, 1745, 1748, 1749, and 1750. Personally I attach no importance to this matter, for it was simply a question of "supply and demand," but, as Bro. Norton chose to make the assertion in order to support his charges against Dermott, and I knew it to be not strictly in accordance with the truth, I felt bound to show him that he was historically wrong. Considering the very great disparity between the Antients and the Moderns at the time the former were trying to "hook" a noble Grand Master, and the prejudice which then existed against the lower class of Irish, of which this body was chiefly composed, the wonder to me is, not that they had some *difficulty* in getting one, but that they ever got one at all; and it is quite evident that Dermott must have used some potent and convincing arguments, or he would never have succeeded either with Lord Blesinton or the other noblemen who followed him ; more especially with the Duke of Athole, who was certainly no soft-hearted greenhorn such as Bro. Norton would have us believe was the case with Lord Blesinton, but which I must beg leave to doubt, for when elected Grand Master he was 47 years old, already a Past Grand Master of Ireland, and was *created a peer* in 1745.

I was under the impression that I had effectually disposed of the unfounded and malicious partizan concoctions of Heseltine and Preston, but I was evidently mistaken, for Bro. Norton appears to have swallowed these slanders as certain small animals are said to devour the compounds artfully prepared for their destruction, *i.e.,* "with avidity," although he will not believe a single word of the other side of the story.

He *has* condescended to admit the *possibility* that Lord Blesinton " was induced, *more or less reluctantly,* to yield to Dermott's solicitation, *which he soon after regretted. Anyhow, he seems to have been ashamed of his new connections, for he never went near them, and was anxious to cast himself loose from Dermott and Co.* " That such was the case may be inferred from the following extract from a letter of Brother Heseltine, Grand

L I

Secretary of England, dated 1769." *   Here, again, Bro.
Norton has allowed his imagination far too much play,
and, as on previous occasions, it has prompted him to
make assertions for which he has no authority, and
which are directly opposed to evidence.   There cannot
be, in my opinion, the shadow of a doubt that Lord
Blesinton *was* Grand Master of the Antients from
1756 to 1760, for the "Transactions" of the Grand
Lodge show that he was regularly elected and proclaimed
every year, with his own permission, until the 24th
December, 1760, when, at a Grand Lodge of Emergency,
the Deputy Grand Master announced that " his Lordship
had signified his desire of quitting the Chair."   The
Earl of Kelly, who had intimated his willingness to
accept the Grand Mastership, was nominated and elected
at the same meeting, and installed on the following St.
John's Day.   There is no evidence, so far as I am aware,
of any " *reluctance* " on the part of Lord Blesinton to
take the Chair, that he ever "regretted" that step, that
he was " ashamed of his new connection," or that he
" was anxious to cast himself loose from Dermott and
Co."   The simple fact that he performed the functions of
Grand Master *longer than any* of his predecessors (with
one exception), either in England, Scotland, or Ireland,
should suffice to dispose of each and all of these
assertions.   And as for his not going " near them," that
does not amount to much, for they evidently went near
enough to *him* to enable him to sign the Warrants and
do anything else that was required.   Bro. Norton is
probably not aware that some of the Grand Masters on
the other side only attended Grand Lodge once during
their term of office; and it may be a matter of surprise
to him to learn that the present M.W. Grand Master of
England has not attended Grand Lodge for several
years—but we do not infer thereby that His Royal
Highness is ashamed of his connection, or that he wishes
"to cast himself loose" from us.   We know perfectly

---

* The letter here referred to is given in Chap. VII. of " Masonic
Facts and Fictions."

well that although our Royal Grand Master does not
often preside in person over our assemblies, he takes a
warm interest in the affairs of the Craft. He signs our
Warrants and other documents—and indeed, does
everything that we can reasonably expect him to do.
We also know that if the Prince of Wales had a desire
to vacate his office he would not hesitate to give effect to
such desire, in the same way as the Earl of Blesinton
might have done had he been so disposed. The exception
to which I have alluded was Lord Byron, who was elected
Grand Master of the Moderns on the 3rd of April, 1747,
and his successor was elected on the 16th March, 1752.
This nobleman attended Grand Lodge three times during
his Grand Mastership, viz., when he was elected, when he
proposed his successor, and at the ensuing Grand Feast. *

I think I have now dealt with nearly all Bro. Norton's
objections; with what success I will leave to the judgment of the candid and impartial reader. I can only say
that my task has been a most agreeable one, for corresponding with him, either privately or publicly, is second
only to the pleasure of meeting and conversing with him,
and if I have not succeeded in knocking over *all* his fads
and fancies I can only express my regret, for I assure
him I meant to do so, and I have done my best. He
must therefore "take the will for the deed." Still, if
there should be any particular subject or question which
he thinks is not quite clear and satisfactory, he has only
to mention it, and I shall be most happy to give it every
attention. In looking over Bro. Norton's "Comments"
to see whether I had left undone anything I ought to have
done I stumbled against his "*whopper,*" on page 242 of
the *Chronicle.* Now, I am not quite sure that Bro.
Norton understands the meaning of the answer to which

* William, fifth Lord Byron, killed William Chaworth, Esq., in a
duel, 26th Jan., 1765, was tried by his peers in Westminster Hall and
found guilty of Manslaughter; but, claiming the benefit of the statute of
Edward VI., he was discharged upon simply paying his fees. He was
great-uncle of the celebrated poet, who succeeded him as sixth Lord
Byron.

he has applied this significant phrase, and if *he* does, probably there are others who do not. I will therefore mention that the key to it may be found on the base of the pedestal which forms the frontispiece of " Masonic Facts and Fictions," and the following explanation is given in the third and all subsequent editions of " Ahiman Rezon ":—" In the queries relative to Antient and Modern Masonry (page xxvi.) the author of ' Ahiman Rezon ' has said that he could convey his mind to an Antient Mason in the presence of a Modern Mason without the latter knowing whether either of them were Masons. He now positively asserts that he is able, with a few Masonic implements, *i.e.*, two squares and a common gavil or hammer, to convey any word or sentence of his own, or the immediate dictations of a stranger, to a skilful or intelligent Freemason of the Antient Order, without speaking, writing or noise ; and that to any distance where the parties can see each other, and at the same time be able to distinguish squares from circles. But, as Mr. Locke observed, this is not the case with all Masons (there were no Modern Masons in his time) ; few of them are acquainted with this secret. The writer of this note has known it for upwards of thirty years, and has never taught it to more than six persons, of which number our Right Worshipful and very worthy Deputy Grand Master, William Dickey, Esq., is one, and Brother Shatwell, the publisher of this book, another."

Doubtless some of my readers are aware that Dermott alludes to what is known as " the Old Masonic Alphabet " (probably a relic of the Operative Masons), the knowledge of which he appears to have been not a little proud of, for he has used it occasionally in his Registers and Minute Books ; but the best specimen of his handiwork of this kind is that previously mentioned on the frontispiece of " Masonic Facts and Fictions." I am inclined to think that it was not so much a mystery to the Moderns as he imagined ; probably it may have gone out of fashion in London, and have been comparatively lost sight of in that neighbourhood. Hence he fancied it was almost restricted to the Society to which he belonged; I have certainly never met with it in either books or documents appertaining to the Moderns, but I have on those belonging to their rivals. This explanation will doubtless render the "*whopper*" less formidable than it appears at first sight.

5.

12th JANUARY, 1889.

IN the concluding portion of Bro. Norton's "Comments" he has alluded to my "good-natured effort of transforming Dermott and his seventy or more associates of 1751 and 1752 into Masonic saints." Now, I am not going to quarrel with him over his little flutter of imagination, but I take this opportunity of assuring him that good nature had nothing whatever to do with my endeavours to put a new complexion on the question of the "Origin of the Antient Grand Lodge," and, between ourselves, I am inclined to think he has paid me an undeserved compliment, for I very much fear that good nature is not one of my weaknesses. It is not an easy task to identify motives for one's own actions, but if I have been at all influenced by sentiment, I think it not unlikely that a love of truth and justice had something to do with my undertaking.

From the very beginning of my Masonic studies I could never quite reconcile myself to the popular and accepted version of the "Origin of the Antients." The whole story bristles with inconsistencies, which no previous writer has explained away—at any rate not to my satisfaction. For the first ray of light I am indebted to my much-esteemed friend and brother, Jacob Norton, of Boston, U.S.A. May I indulge in the hope that henceforth he will remember this fact, and that it will be the means of inducing him to view with a more favourable eye the theory for which, although unintentionally, he is in some degree responsible. Doubtless

this will be *news* to him, but with his wonderful memory I shall have no difficulty in making him understand my meaning. Some years ago, when Bro. Norton was engaged in a controversy with Bro. Hughan or some other Masonic writer, he requested me to search the Grand Lodge records for information bearing on the subject then under discussion, and in doing so I came across the following item in the Minutes of 11th December, 1735:—
"Notice being given to the Grand Lodge that the Master and Wardens of a Lodge from Ireland attended without, desiring to be admitted by virtue of a Deputation from the Lord Kingston, present Grand Master of Ireland. But it appearing there was no particular Recommendation from his Lordship in this affair, their Request could not be complied with unless they would accept of a new Constitution here."

I copied this item and sent it in my next letter to Bro. Norton, with an intimation that I thought it possible that this incident had something to do with the origin of the Antients. My correspondent probably did not see anything in it, for he made no reply to my suggestion; however, he will know from the lapse of time since the correspondence I have alluded to that this theory of mine is not simply an idea of rapid and recent growth; and I am perfectly satisfied that had Bro. Norton or any other of our historians the same facilities for acquiring information, and had given as much consideration to this particular subject as I have, he would have been as convinced as I am of the Irish origin of the Antients, that no secession worthy of the name ever occurred in the history of English Masonry, and that the only branch of the fraternity to which the term " Schismatics " can with propriety be applied is the body of malcontents who associated with Preston in his abortive attempt to establish a schismatic Grand Lodge in the latter part of the last century.

Now, although Bro. Norton is absolutely silent on this non-secession theory, which really occupies about three-fourths of the book he has been criticising, he has said that he believes Heseltine's description of the Antients, notwithstanding the evidence I have adduced as to its incredibility, and the indisputable fact that the letter he refers to was written with no other object than to depreciate a successful rival Society ; hence, I may assume that he does not accept my theory, for if he believes Heseltine and Preston's version it is quite evident he cannot believe mine. I wish particularly to have Bro. Norton's opinion on the Irish evidence contained in Chapter V. of " Masonic Facts and Fictions," but before he gives it it is only fair that I should mention that I do not imagine there is nothing more to be said, either for or against my views and the evidence set forth in the chapter indicated. The more I learn, and the more I think about this matter, the more firmly convinced am I that the theory I have offered is the only feasible solution of a question which has puzzled all our most thoughtful writers. I have never met with this incident of the refusal to admit the Irish Masons to Grand Lodge in print until it was mentioned in Gould's History of Freemasonry, and although the author does not appear to attach particular importance to it, he says :—" It is a little singular that in 1735, whilst this nobleman was at the head of the Craft in Ireland, the Master and Wardens of an *Irish* Lodge were refused admission to the Grand Lodge of *England* ‘ unless ’—to quote from the records —‘ they would accept of a new Constitution here.’ " * It will be seen that there exists a slight verbal difference between Bro. Gould's description and my extract from the records, for the former reads thus—" the Master and Wardens of an *Irish* Lodge," while the latter reads —" The Master and Wardens of a Lodge *from* Ireland." Now, I always thought this *very* singular, and I thus refer to it on page 127 of " Masonic Facts and Fictions," " bearing in mind the fact that the nobleman mentioned had only a few years before (1728-9) presided over their own Grand Lodge with much *éclat*,

---

* Lord Kingston is the nobleman referred to.

and had also made them several valuable presents ; this
proceeding seems as churlish, as it was certainly short-
sighted, on the part of the 'regulars.' Private Lodges
would, of course, take their cue from the Grand Lodge,
and refuse to open their doors to these strangers whose
working was different to theirs."

"Does any one at all familiar with the characteristics
of an Irishman imagine that 'Pat' would meekly submit
to such treatment ? If he does, I most decidedly do not.
It seems to me much more likely that he would call some
of his countrymen about him and open a Lodge on his
own account, or 'by virtue' of the before-mentioned
Deputation or Warrant, for we must remember that
exclusive Masonic jurisdiction' was unknown at this
period. One Lodge would, of course, beget others, and
so it probably went on until unconstituted Masonic
Lodges became the rallying points or centres of union
of nearly all the Irish mechanics and labourers that came
over to seek employment in the English metropolis."
"The migratory character of this class will, I think,
sufficiently account for the comparatively small number
to be found on the register at the formation of their
Grand Lodge, also for the rapid growth of their provincial
and military Lodges. This was my opinion in 1887 ;
since then I have read something which has induced me
to review this subject, and although it has not led to any
material alteration of opinion it has opened up fresh
ground and furnished additional food for reflection. In
"The Cabinet History of England," written by Charles
Macfarlane and published by Blackie and Son, on page 31,
Volume 16, will be found the following paragraph :—
"The gin mobs were not yet tranquilized, *and other riots
were caused in London by the employment in the Spitalfields looms of a number of poor Irish who had come over
to mow and reap, but who had engaged to help to weave
silk at two-thirds of the ordinary wages.*" I may observe
that the writer of the foregoing paragraph is describing
the condition of London and the difficulties of the
Government in the year 1736; and when viewed in

conjunction with the incident of the 11th December of the previous year, it appears to me to furnish a very probable explanation of the action of the Grand Lodge; that is supposing these strangers to have been merely travelling Masons, or " sojourners " as they would then be called; *popular prejudice* would doubtless not be without its effect on the officials, but even this does not satisfactorily account for the alternative, "unless they would accept of a *new* Constitution here."

In referring to the early records of the Grand Lodge of England, on page 22 of "Masonic Facts and Fictions" I have said—" every line is worthy of careful consideration, and that there is evidently more in these transactions than appears upon the surface," and it seems to me that these words are especially applicable to the record I have just quoted. At first sight the impression left on my mind was that the passage referred to the Master and Wardens of an *Irish Lodge, i.e.*, a Lodge *in* Ireland, but further consideration has resulted in my putting another construction upon it, viz., that these brethren were officers of a Lodge then actually meeting in London "by virtue of a Deputation (or Dispensation) from the Lord Kingston," who, as before stated, was a Past Grand Master of England, and I should say deservedly popular during his Grand Mastership. On page 33 I have given one instance of a Past Grand Master of England constituting a Lodge some years after he had ceased his connection with the Grand Lodge, and although it is possible that this particular " Deputation " *may* have been issued for a Lodge to meet in Ireland, I think it much more likely that it was a sort of a " roving Commission," authorising the holders to meet as a Lodge wherever they thought proper. This appears to me the most reasonable construction that can be put upon the incident, for it will account for the officers of " a Lodge *from* Ireland " being together in attendance at the very same meeting of the Grand Lodge, their being denied admission, the alternative offered them, and the reference to the " Deputation."

Bro. Norton appears to have but a poor opinion of my method of arriving at conclusions, viz.: " by reading something here and something there "—and I admit that it is sometimes rather a tedious process ; yet I think it preferable to the acrobatic performance known as " *jumping* at conclusions," which, although possibly more expeditious, occasionally results in the discomfiture of the jumper ; I shall therefore go on in my old way of " putting this and that together," and trust to his intelligence and good nature to do the best he can with the whole.

I would first ask him to bear in mind the quotation from the " History of England," and then turn to page 82 of " Masonic Facts," &c., where he may find mention of a complaint made in the Grand Committee of the Antients by " John Robinson, of No. 9, against Moses Willoughby, of the same Lodge, for defrauding him of nine shillings in a bargain in the exchanging of a *loomb*." This matter had been referred to a Committee of *weavers*, " who had decided against the defendant, and he was ordered to refund the money on pain of expulsion ; but Moses was a hardened sinner. ' He declared they might expel him, for he would not conform to the Rules of any Society upon Earth by which he should loose nine shillings. Therefore he was Unanimously Expelled, and deem'd unworthy of this or any other good Society.' "

This important matter had probably been in dispute for some time, for the minutes of the Grand Committee of 3rd June, 1752, contain " *a formal* Complaint, by Bro. John Robinson," to the above purport, and the committee of investigation was then appointed, consisting of " Thomas Kane, Thomas O'hara, and John Morris, all Weavers, and of the said Lodge, No. 9."

The first-named brother appears in Morgan's Register as " Thomas Kaan, Weaver, residing in Brick Lane " (Spitalfields). He is No. 117 on the list. Thomas O'Harah (O'hara) is No. 50 on the list and his residence is " Opposite ye Two Brewers, Brick Lane,

Spitalfields." When this brother joined, or was *made*, I have no means of ascertaining, for he was one of the original members, *i.e.*, one of those who belonged to the Society on the 17th July, 1751. and John Morris is No. 58 on the list—same address as the last-named brother. While on the subject of this old register, which I consider the most valuable of all the records of the Antients for my present purpose, I may mention that out of the first 200 names only about 140 have the "place of abode and occupation" appended. As may be imagined, nearly every trade and calling is represented; but I notice that the weaving class predominates, there being out of the 140 about 21 that come under this designation, and about 35 of the 140 are said to reside in Spitalfields and the immediate neighbourhood. Doubtless Bro. Norton will consider these *facts* deserving of attention, although there is a lapse of 15 or 16 years between the period at which I place the commencement of the Antient *régime* (about 1735) and the date of their consolidation as an organized Society, but only about four or five between Preston's earliest date (1739) and mine. That I quite concur with Bro. Norton in his estimate of the character of James Heseltine will be seen by a reference to page 182 of "Facts and Fictions," but that he "had good reason to despise Dermott." or even that he *did* despise him, I may be permitted to doubt. I think, as a general rule, people are not disposed to write long letters about those whom they despise, although they sometimes do so when *fear* is the motive power. My old friend seems to have lost sight of the fact that Heseltine was a lawyer, and that he "held a brief for the other side," and also that the greater part of the letter of which he thinks so highly was of the " some one told me somebody said " character, for the writer of it had only been a Mason about four years, and Grand Secretary *not as many months*. He says the late Bro. Revis told him that Lord Blesinton had forbidden the Antients to use his name as their Grand Master, and Bro. Norton believes that Revis *did* give him this information; so do I, but that

Revis " told the truth " is, to say the least of it, doubtful. What I want to know is—Why this brother, who was Grand Secretary from 1734 to 1756, did not at the same time tell him how and when the people he was reviling seceded ? That he did not do so is quite evident, for " the words *seceders* or *schismatics* are not to be found in this long and carefully-written document, nor does the writer even insinuate that these terms might with propriety be applied to them.

" He says they '*first made their appearance about the year 1746.*'" Do these words indicate secession ? I think not. In my opinion their meaning is clear and conclusive, viz., that these people "*made their appearance*" from some other quarter. Heseltine was not the man to have neglected this most effective of weapons had he known, or even thought of, its existence ; it was reserved for the more clever but less scrupulous Preston to concoct and propagate this stigma. I have shown that in 1766 a member of the Antient fraternity was described in a Minute Book of the rival Society as an "*Irish York Mason*"—in 1776 the Antients were described by a distinguished Masonic author as "*the Irish Faction,* ye A.M.'s as they call themselves "; in 1786 their Warrants were referred to as "*Irish* Warrants "; in 1793 their Lodges were designated "*Irish,*" and in a pamphlet printed in 1806 they are called "*Irishmen.*" I will now add that since my book was publishd I have seen their lodges mentioned in another pamphlet, printed in 1766, as "*Irish Lodges.*" And these terms have all been applied by different persons, totally unconnected, and uninfluenced by any sinister motive. I shall be very much obliged if Bro. Norton will give me his opinion on the foregoing points. If not troubling him too much, I should also like to know his explanation of the reason of a large majority of the Antients on their first register being Irishmen, and, without going into further details, how he can account for the numerous points of resemblance between the Irish fraternity and the Antients in England to which I have drawn attention. How it was that the customs, ceremonial and otherwise, of the latter were totally different to those of the body from which they are said to have seceded, and how he accounts for the persistent ignoring of the Moderns by the Grand Lodges of Scotland and Ireland; those bodies having been from the first in close alliance with the *despised* and *so-called* " Schismatics."

6.

19th JANUARY, 1889.

IN my last contribution I expressed a wish for Bro. Norton's opinion on certain points relative to the no-secession theory propounded in "Masonic Facts and Fictions," and as I have no desire to overcrowd him with work I will reserve a few others until he has had time to " consider and report " on those already mentioned; indeed, it will in some measure depend upon the nature of his reply whether I trouble him again on this subject. It may be, and I hope it will, that on the main question we agree, and if so I have very little more to say, for if it be any satisfaction to him I will readily concede that the " so-called Antients " were not entitled to that distinctive appellation according to the general acceptation of the term in the present day. In my opinion, this phase of the subject is hardly worth serious discussion, for, after all, it must be admitted that the word " ancient " is not arbitrary, and was often used to denote something old, *i.e.*, not *new* or *modern*, as

A very *ancient* and fish-like smell.
I will feed fat the *ancient* grudge I bear him.

Surely my old friend will not deny that Dermott and his party were perfectly justified in adhering to the description given of them by the highest authority in the ranks of their opponents, no other than Dr. Anderson, to whom I have already given credit for having first used the words " antient " and " modern " in relation to Freemasonry. On page 96 of the Constitutions of 1738 will be found the paragraph quoted by Bro. Norton in his article of the 20th October, commencing "At last the antient Fraternity of Free and Accepted Masons in *Ireland*," which he has attributed to "the editor of the Dublin Constitutions of 1751," but which really emanated from *our own* learned historian, and was simply copied verbatim by Bro. Spratt, as was nearly the whole of his book. I do think, therefore, that the anger of my friendly critic is misplaced in saying "they had no right to pretend to antiquity or to the name of Antients," and that he is unnecessarily severe upon the "seventy or eighty members" who in 1751 decided to organize and consolidate for their mutual benefit; and as this great and learned authority saw no impropriety in applying the term "modern" to his own party in the same book in 1738, I fail to see any reason why we of the present day should be either surprised or annoyed with others for so describing it a few years later. I have already noted several instances of the application of the term "modern" to their own Society by the adherents of the Grand Lodge of 1717, and I *could* mention others if necessary; the fact is they were so designated in printed books as well as in written letters, and in my opinion no objection would ever have been raised to it had not the authorities discovered that it was a source of weakness to them, and that their rivals were getting the best of the battle for supremacy.

I sincerely hope Bro. Norton has no fault to find with my method of replying to his "Comments"—that he has not taken offence where none was intended, for I assure him I have endeavoured to control, as far as possible, my natural propensity for saying things unpalatable; and if I have occasionally indulged in a little mild banter, or a small joke at his expense, I trust he will not bear malice on that score, but will permit me to plead in extenuation "that I really couldn't help it, and it was only a *very little* one after all." Besides, I may remind him that the book is my "first-born." Some little allowance, therefore, ought to be made for parental pride as well as for natural affection, and as Bro Norton well knows a father's protection is of the highest value to his offspring in their early days, he but ill discharges the duties of a parent who sends them prematurely out to battle with this hard censorious world without being prepared to defend them should occasion demand it. Now I have every reason to be satisfied with this child of mine. He is doing very well at present, and although only a little over twelve months old he has got several teeth, and takes quite naturally to the toughest of crusts. He will, I hope, shortly be able to run alone, and even fight his own battles. Until he is able to do so I shall certainly do my best to protect him against all attacks from whatever quarter they may come. I am unaware of the actual number of brethren across the Atlantic who hold the same views as Bro. Norton with regard to "Masonic Facts and Fictions," but there is certainly *one* besides himself. If, therefore, he thinks I have at any time hit him too hard, he has only to remember that a blow loses much of its force by expansion or distribution, and if he will share it with his colleague, and do so with his usual liberality, he will scarcely feel its effects himself. I now allude to the editor of the "Keystone," Philadelphia, who says in that journal of the third of November last: " Bro. Jacob Norton of Boston 'does not agree' with Bro. Sadler in his 'Facts and Fictions.' In other words, he thinks his facts are fiction and his fiction facts. Bro. Norton 'shake,' since for once we are agreed." I hope that "shake" has come off, and that it has been a source of mutual enjoyment to the parties concerned. If the writer intended this paragraph as a gratuitous advertisement I am extremely obliged to him, and if it was meant merely as a sample of Yankee smartness he is heartily welcome to all the credit he is likely to get by it. Some people have found Bro. Norton alone *quite* enough to tackle single-handed, and it would have been perhaps as *well* to have heard the other side before coming to a decision. However, as our brother has thought proper to rush

M

uninvited to the fray, he will, I doubt not, readily divide
the spoils of the battle with his companion in arms.
Whenever I hear the words "Masonry unites men of
every country, sect, and opinion" I shall be reminded of
the wonder worked by my little book in reconciling two
distinguished members of our Order, who *never had*
agreed before, and the picture of Bro. Norton and his
life-long antagonist fraternising and shaking, *actually
shaking,* over "Masonic Facts and Fictions" will amply
repay me for all my trouble in writing the book, and be
a consolation in my darkest hours. Kicking a dead
man is a comparatively safe and easy mode of fighting,
but at best it can only result in an inglorious victory.
Now, if these valiant champions are not yet satisfied, I
shall at any time be most happy to "run a tilt" with
them, either in defence of the memory of Laurence
Dermott, or of my own arguments in "Masonic Facts
and Fictions." I am almost as much in the dark as to
the number of unbelievers in my new theory to be found
in this country, but I will take this opportunity for
mentioning a few who did or do believe in it, and
whose opinions should have some weight. Amongst
the former, I am happy in being able to include the
late Rev. A. F. A. Woodford, Past Grand Chaplain of
England, for many years editor of the *Freemason,* and
every one who knew *him* must admit that he would not
readily abandon an old tradition unless perfectly satisfied
that it had no foundation, nor adopt a new theory unless
convinced of its soundness. It affords me much pleasure
to record the fact that a favourable view of my theory
has been expressed by Sir Albert W. Woods, C.B.,
Garter, King of Arms, P.G.W., &c., who has held the office
of Grand Director of Ceremonies for thirty years out of
his forty as a Mason. Bro. F. A. Philbrick, Q.C., Grand
Registrar of England, says, "You have, I think, made
out your case ; you have put it very clearly and suc-
cinctly, and have carried conviction to my mind. . . . .
Your success is not only gratifying as showing a desire
to get at the truth in the Craft, but also a testimony

to the fairness and ability with which the work has been executed."

The opinion of Bro. Thomas Fenn, President of the Board of General Purposes, can be seen in the Preface of the book; and Colonel Shadwell H. Clerke, Grand Secretary of England, has given me permission to say that he is fully satisfied that my theory is correct. The brethren I have named are not at all likely to have been influenced by merely personal considerations, and were it necessary, or even deemed advisable, I could mention a large number of others who hold similar opinions.

I am sorry I cannot include some of my most esteemed brothers of the pen; however, I do not despair even in that quarter, for "*time* is on my side." Indeed, it would have been little short of a miracle if I had succeeded in one single effort in convincing every one of our historians that they have been wrong on this question all their lives. The difficulty of my task may be well illustrated by the following anecdote.

While the compilation of "Masonic Facts, &c.," was in progress, I accidentally met with one of our most cautious and experienced Masonic authors, and, wishing to ascertain his views on the subject, I mildly asked, "Did you ever hear of any other theory for the origin of the Antients than that of secession from the regular Grand Lodge?" He was utterly astounded at the absurdity of the question, and when he had sufficiently recovered I found it necessary to explain; ultimately he *did* grasp my meaning, and his answer was, "of *course* not, why they *must* have seceded—where could they have come from if they did not?" For certain private reasons I did not deem it worth while to discuss the question contained in his answer, and I think from that time the subject has never been mentioned between us.

M I

7.

30th MARCH, 1889.

APART from the admission that Bro. Norton was wrong in accusing Laurence Dermott of being a forger as well as a fool, I see very little in his article of the 9th February that has not appeared in his previous "Comments," and has been dealt with to the best of my ability.

I shall not, therefore, waste time by any further attempts to refute the stale slanders and unfounded assertions which form its distinguishing features.

The imputation of being "infatuated with Dermottism, etc.," and that I have worked myself "into a mere partizan of Dermott and Co.," has not up to the time present disturbed my rest in the smallest degree, for, without searching the pages of "Masonic Facts and Fictions," I feel sure there is nothing therein to render such an assertion justifiable. I simply look upon it as one of those fanciful flights of imagination so common to a great genius, and especially so to Bro. Jacob Norton, being one of the most characteristic and attractive features of his contributions to Masonic literature.

In reply to the continued animadversions on the adoption by Dermott of the title "Antient York Masons," I can only repeat that I fail to see why Bro. Norton should be so very angry with Dermott for having utilised this little scrap of Masonic history in the way he did, bearing in mind that, from the days of Anderson down to the present time, we have been taught to believe that we are all descendants of the Masons who held the first Grand Lodge at York in the year 926.

It seems to me that the proper person on whom to vent his spleen would be the father of Masonic historians, Anderson, as he appears to have been the first to promulgate the story. Whether Dermott is deserving of praise or censure for having brought it more prominently before the brotherhood is a mere matter of opinion, and notwithstanding the severity of Bro. Norton's remarks I still think that a certain amount of credit is due to his forethought in this matter. I should be exceedingly reluctant to say that Bro. Norton is a victim to blind partizanship and unreasonable prejudice, but perhaps he can explain how it is that he has not a word of condemnation for Heseltine, Grand Secretary of the Moderns, the writer of the letter on page 179 of " Facts and Fictions," wherein he says:—"The Society of Ancient York Masons, under Direction of the G.L., was Transferred many years ago to London. . . . . " Upon the whole, Sir, your Lodge will no doubt discover the total fallacy of Mr. Law. Dermott's account, and that ours is the real Ancient Grand Lodge of York . . . ." and Preston, their historian, who says: "Under the fictitious sanction of the Ancient York Constitution, which was *entirely dropt at the revival* of the Grand Lodge in 1717 . . . ."

Now, to my thinking, Dermott's offence, assuming it to have been an offence, when compared with these palpable falsehoods, is of the mildest description, but the authors of them were the opponents of Dermott, consequently Bro. Norton believes in them ; they have " found favour in his sight." although he " disbelieves anything and everything that was written by Dermott." He will not even accept the explanation given in "Ahiman Rezon," probably in reply to some Jacob Norton of the 18th century.

" They are called York Masons, because the first Grand Lodge in England was congregated at York, A.D. 926."

I cannot pass over, without an appearance of disrespect which I am far from feeling, the paragraph which contains the opinion of my redoubtable opponent on the " seventy worthies immortalized by the pen of John Morgan in 1751." I make 78 of them, but a few more or less is not a matter of importance, since Brother Norton believes " that every one of them were initiated in regular chartered Lodges, either in England, Ireland, or elsewhere." I am inclined to think this *belief* will not be shared by many of the readers of the *Chronicle*, in the face of the following declaration, copied from Morgan's Register, and printed on pp. 76-77 of " Masonic Facts and Fictions," with the names of the Masters, Wardens, and Past Masters of seven Lodges who were present at the time it was writton :—

> And whereas several of the Lodges have congregated and made Masons without any Warrant (not with a desire of Acting wrong, but thro: the Necessity above mention'd), in order to Rectify such irregular proceedings (as far as in our power) it is hereby Order'd That the Grand Secretary shall write Warrants (on Parchment) for the Unwarranted Lodges, viz., The Lodges known by the Title of No. 2, 3, 4, 5, 6, and that all the said Warrants shall bear date July the Seventeenth One thousand Seven hundred fifty and One being the day on which the said Lodges met (at the Turk's head Tavern, in Greek-street, Soho), to revive the Ancient Craft.

That some of these original members were initiated in regular Lodges under the Grand Lodge of Ireland is evinced by the Records, but that fact does not, in my opinion, warrant their being branded as " rebels," " schismatics," and " seceders" from the Grand Lodge of England, although according to the peculiar mode of reasoning adopted by Bro. Norton and certain other of my critics they fully deserved these titles.

The choice collection of contemptuous epithets which my opponent so lavishly and indiscriminately hurls at his Masonic ancestors forcibly reminds me of an old saying, " It is an ill bird that befouls its own nest." I should have thought that respect, if not affection, for his "own dear mother Lodge" would have induced him to use milder and more appropriate language when referring to the body from which it emanated than " riff-raff," " scum," " charlatans," " scalawags," and " perjurers."

It is not for me to dictate to him any particular mode of discussing this question, yet, as an expression of opinion only, I think he might well have been content with the true description given by me of the organizers of the Antient Grand Lodge, viz., that they consisted chiefly of Irish mechanics and labourers, neither better nor worse than the same class in the present day. This, in my opinion, accounts at once for the absence of stability with regard to their *five* original Lodges, which seems to puzzle him considerably, and for which he can find no better explanation than the " ignorance of their members." The absurdity of Bro. Norton's concluding paragraphs is on a par with the cool assurance of his extraordinary proposal. For my own part, I am inclined to think that my old friend is indulging in a little pleasantry at my expense. Should I, however, be mistaken, and he is really serious, I will tell him that, so far as I am personally concerned, he may at once abandon all hope that I shall accede to his preposterous recommendation unless something more reliable and tangible than his " belief" can be adduced in support of it ; and as for the Masons of Antient descent (of whom I am proud of being one), I have no doubt they are well able to take care of their own interests— quite as capable, indeed, as were their forefathers in 1813. Still, as Bro. Norton appears to feel strongly on this matter, I would suggest that he tries the effect of his new doctrine on his " own dear mother Lodge," which is about to celebrate its Centenary. I make no doubt that he would have a hearty welcome, and that his proposal would receive all the consideration its importance and originality merits.

Bro. Norton's proposal, which I have dubbed preposterous, was the following :—" That Bro. Sadler should use his talent and influence to enlighten the prominent members of the ' Grand Masters' Lodge,' and of all other Lodges who hold Charters from the so-called Antients, including my own dear ' Mother Lodge ' —viz., that of ' Joppa '—that, however blameless they were for the sins committed by their Masonic forefathers of 1751, they are, nevertheless, not justified in retaining the usurped ranks on the list of Lodges unjustly wrenched by their predecessors in 1813 from the Lodge of Antiquity and all other Lodges that were chartered before 1752 by the Grand Lodge of England. It is, therefore, the bounden duty of all Masons of the Ancients' lineage or descent to ask the Grand Lodge to renumber her Lodges, and to have each Lodge placed on the list in accordance with the priority of their respective dates of Constitution.

"And, second, as the word 'United,' which was forced upon the Grand Lodge in 1813, serves merely as a reminder of the rascality perpetrated by former unworthy Masons, the said word should therefore at once be stricken out, so that the title of the Grand Lodge may be restored to what it was before 1813.

" I will only add that by doing what is above recommended great credit will be reflected upon the character of English Masons and Masonry in general, but more especially so on those brethren of Antients' descent, who would cheerfully and voluntarily surrender to the proper and legal owners what they were unjustly deprived of in 1813."

I come now to Bro. Norton's article of 9th of March, and I trust he will pardon me if I do not give as much attention to each paragraph as he may think it deserves ; the fact is, I am now closely occupied with other matters, which cannot well be deferred.

I have first to thank him most sincerely for his endeavours to clear away the dust with which he says I have unintentionally bespattered the eyes of my readers. I was not aware that I had done anything of the kind, having heard no complaints of that nature on this side of the Atlantic, where I may fairly assume that a great majority of the readers of the *Chronicle* are to be found. If, however, I have been so unfortunate, I can only say that I am exceedingly sorry for it, and I hope that the efforts of Bro. Norton have been completely successful. My explanation of the sentence quoted by Bro. Norton from page 130 of " Facts and Fictions " is, that it formed a portion of my remarks on the Grand Lodge *Seals* of the Antients, their Warrants being mentioned elsewhere, and that is why the words " *complete* Warrant" were used. If Bro. Norton considers a Warrant *complete* without the Grand Lodge seal, I have only to say that I do not. I am therefore under the necessity of reminding him that by omitting the word "complete" he did *not* repeat what I had printed, his words being: "Bro. Sadler, however, never saw a Warrant of the Antients older than 1772"; whereas, in another part of the book, I had stated that I had two older ones before me—viz., one of 1757 and the other of 1759.

I beg to apologise to Bro. Norton for having misunderstood his reference to the Nova Scotian documents, which I have never seen, and he has not at hand to refer to. I have looked over his "Comments" again, and I imagine I must have been misled by the following sentence: "Both documents are headed with 'Blesinton,' but neither of them are signed by the Grand Master, but by 'Lau. Dermott, G. Sec.' The question, therefore, is —did Lord Blessington ever sign a Warrant at all?" Now, as the foregoing is a portion of the lengthy accusation against Dermott of having forged the signature of the Grand Master, I think Bro. Norton will admit that my mistake was not an unnatural one. However, I accept with pleasure his disclaimer that he did not accuse Dermott of having committed forgeries for "exportation," but merely for "home consumption." Notwithstanding Bro. Norton's recent explanation, I must confess to being still somewhat hazy with regard to these documents, which he says are headed "Blesinton," and yet not signed by that nobleman, but by Dermott; and I think it not at all unlikely that if I could but get a sight of them I should come to the conclusion that they bear the actual signature of the Grand Master, as well as that of the Grand Secretary.

I am delighted to find that there is at last a prospect of a change of employment for me, and that instead of defending the Antients from the abuse which has been so freely showered upon them, I have now before me the much more congenial task of defending my own writings.

I have first to thank Bro. Norton for taking the trouble to point out the "mistakes in 'Facts and

Fictions' "; it is what I have asked several of my friends to do, for however careful one may be, errors *will* occasionally creep in, but up to now I have had to make very few corrections. Various kinds of mistakes are to be met with in literary productions. There is the writer's mistake, the printer's mistake, and occasionally a mistake is made by the reader, but as a matter of course this rarely happens. It seems to me, however, that the "mistakes" to which Bro. Norton directs attention will be more easily found in his own fertile imagination than in the book he fancies he is criticising. For instance, I should like to know on what page he finds the first mistake, "Bro. Sadler claims that the Installation ceremony with word, grip, &c., was designed by Anderson, to be repeated after every election of a new Master for an old Lodge." To the best of my knowledge, I have not made any such claim. I certainly did not mention "grip, word, &c.," nor did I state that the ceremony "was designed by Anderson." What I *did* say will be found on page 196, and is as follows :—

If in addition to the foregoing we take into account the abolition of the ceremony of Installation (also enjoined and partly described in the Constitutions of 1723), and the important alterations made in other ceremonies. I think we must admit, that after the year last mentioned the adherents of the regular Grand Lodge had done much to merit the distinctive title of "Modern Masons," the justice of which they tacitly acknowledged, as the records of the Lodge of Promulgation testify. Whereas the rival body having kept alive and continued to observe so many of the old customs of the Order, had a stronger title to the appellation of Antients than has generally been accorded them.

Having gone very fairly and fully into this question of the installation ceremony in my previous replies to Bro. Norton, I have too much regard for the patience of the readers of the *Chronicle* to traverse the same ground again ; I shall therefore content myself with an appeal to their judgment, whether what Bro. Norton *believes*, what he feels *satisfied of*, what he has *no doubt of*, and what he considers he is *justified in inferring*, ought to be received as *evidence* of a mistake on my part ?

8.

6th APRIL, 1889.

MY second mistake may be placed in the same category as my first, for I cannot find it in the book. However, here is a description of it; so perhaps my readers will be more successful :—

"Second, with regard to the transposition of certain words, *I have reason to believe* that as late as 1742 no change was made by the Grand Lodge of England, *nor do I believe* that the Grand Lodge ever authorised any such change. I have, however, sent some hints to an English brother, which *may prove* that the change originated in France. . . . ." I will now summarise as briefly as possible what I have said on this subject. In the year 1730 a pamphlet was published by one Pritchard, purporting to be an exposure of Masonry, containing the ceremonies, &c. This pamphlet is mentioned in the minutes of the Grand Lodge at the time, and it appears to have occasioned much anger and excitement amongst the members. Certain resolutions were passed, with a view of discountenancing impostors and preventing false brethren from gaining admission to the Lodges.

In my opinion, the pamphlet previously noticed coincides with the written minutes of Grand Lodge, which the author is not likely to have seen, and as there is no apparent motive for the invention of the story, I say it is "reasonable, and therefore not inconsistent with truth." Bro. Norton doubtless considers the written records of Grand Lodge and a printed book, open to the whole world, as of no account whatever, for he does not even mention them; but what has he to offer in opposition to this *evidence?* "I have reason to believe," . . . . "nor do I believe," . . . . "I have no doubt," . . . &c. Surely he cannot expect the readers of the *Chronicle* to believe that in the year 1889 he knows more about these matters than one whose acquaintance with Masonry began in 1758, and yet it appears very much like it.

I have searched most carefully through the remainder of Bro. Norton's article for my third mistake, but, as he has omitted to indicate its locality, I am as much in the dark as I was with regard to the preceding ones. I will, however, take the liberty of correcting one or two little mistakes on his part, notwithstanding that this phase of the subject was, in my opinion, fairly and exhaustively dealt with in my article of 12th January last. Being well aware that "argument seldom convinces anyone contrary to his inclination," I shall restrict myself to the task of pointing out, as briefly as possible, the *mistakes* of my corrector.

First, the Resolution of 1724, relating to the admission of visitors, clearly applies to Private Lodges only, and is therefore not applicable to the case of the Irish Masons who desired to be admitted to Grand Lodge in 1735.

Bro. Norton's elaborate explanation seems to me quite superfluous, and not strictly impartial. I prefer the text in its native simplicity. These brethren were refused admission because they were not members of an English Lodge, but they would have been admitted had they consented to "accept of a new Constitution here" (and pay two guineas for it). Consequently the *law* of 1724 had nothing whatever to do with the incident.

It is perfectly well known to Bro. Norton and to all Masonic students, that the "Deputation" mentioned was a document empowering the holders to meet and work as Masons; in fact, only another name for a Constitution, or Warrant.

For these people to carry about with them, in addition to this official document, a written or "Particular recommendation" from their Grand Master, would be, to my thinking, a most extraordinary and unlikely proceeding.

I do *not* say that the Grand Lodge was "Irish-hating," "unjust," "bad," or "heartless." All this must be ascribed to Bro. Norton's exuberance of language and liveliness of imagination.   This is what I *do* say:—

Now, bearing in mind the fact that the nobleman mentioned had only a few years before (1728-9) presided over their own Grand Lodge with much *éclat*, and had also made them several valuable presents, this proceeding seems as churlish as it was certainly short-sighted on the part of the regulars.

Bro. Norton knows perfectly well—no one better— that it is simply impossible for me to produce "*evidence* that either Morgan, Dermott, or any other of the founders of the Antients' concern in 1751 had ever heard about" the affair of 1735. I might with equal reason challenge him to produce evidence that they had *not* heard of it, but I really cannot at present see how such evidence would affect the question of secession.

I should be glad to know on what page of the book I stated that the Grand Lodge had "changed its ceremonies or ritual for the purpose of *excluding* Irish Masons from joining or visiting English Lodges?" I am under the impression that I attributed these alterations chiefly to the fear of Prichard's pamphlet, and I think if my critic reads again the portion of the book from which he has culled the "truly astonishing" quotation, he will readily perceive that the "particular class" referred to was the "*Society* element," or, as Anderson has it, "the better sort," and that it was social condition, not nationality, that I had in my mind when writing it.

Bro. Norton cannot "see any connection between the riots of the Spitalfields weavers in 1736, on account of the Irish competition with them in their trade, with the doings of the Grand Lodge in 1735, or with the doings of Morgan and Co. in 1751." Doubtless, also, in his sweet simplicity and trustful innocence, he has not the remotest idea that these riots were probably attended by "hatred, malice, and all uncharitableness," and that "No Irish need apply" is not unlikely to have been the "shiboleth" of Masons as well as non-Masons in London at that period. Neither can he see anything at all remarkable in the fact of so large a number of the Spitalfields weaving fraternity being on the register of the Antients fifteen years later. I can only say that his mental blindness elicits my sincere pity, and excites my warmest sympathy. It is a curious coincidence, to say the least of it, and in my opinion this circumstance alone indicates pretty clearly the origin of the so-called " Seceders."

Possibly it may never have occurred to Bro. Norton that to raise the comparatively large sum of two guineas amongst these "poor Irish" to pay for a Warrant or Constitution might have been somewhat difficult in those days, even if they had been inclined to accept one.

As the article of 16th March chiefly consists of a repetition of the " mud-slinging " substitute for argument and evidence previously referred to I am not disposed to spend much time over it. I will, however, remind my opponent that even should he succeed in making everybody believe that the Antients merited the opprobrium which he delights in showering upon them, he will be as far off as ever from disproving my facts or discrediting my theory: indeed, he will have rendered me some little service by confirming what I have already stated—that they were a totally different and distinct class of people from the general body of the Moderns, and therefore not likely to have been members of their Lodges.

I am highly delighted and much flattered at finding that Bro. Norton has followed the advice given in one of my former papers; he has been studying *Irish;* although, judging from the result. he does not appear to have made much progress. No doubt he will improve if he goes on and gives his mind to it, but at present his knowledge of the subject appears to partake of a somewhat superficial character. I allude to his classi-fication of the names of the members of the first five Lodges in Morgan's Register, and without entering upon a critical examination of his premises and con-clusions, by means of which he tries to convince us that the English outnumbered the Irish by more than two to one, I shall merely say that I have no faith in his knowledge of Irish names nor in his mode of dealing with the subject. If he refers to pp. 124-5-6 of " Facts and Fictions " he will at once observe that I have not lost sight of the importance of this phase of the question, and that I have arrived at a totally different result by a much more reliable test than that adopted by him ; for whereas he trusted entirely to his superficial knowledge of Irish names and his own prejudiced imagination, my conclusion is based on an examination of two small Irish Directories, the oldest I could find in the British Museum, with the following result :—

Having copied the first hundred names in the register, I found no less than seventy-two similar names in the small directories or almanacks before mentioned—and this during a very hurried examination only— amongst the shop-keeping, manufacturing, and artizan classes of Dublin and Belfast, and I have every reason to believe that had the names of all been correctly spelt by the Grand Secretary the proportion would have been still greater ; also that a corresponding average would be found to exist all through the first register. It will thus be seen that there were good grounds for the ' Ancients ' being afterwards denomi- nated ' *Irish Masons*.' A more recent examination of Directories, &c., in the Dublin and Belfast Libraries has enabled me to reduce the number of unidentified names in the first hundred to eleven, viz., Abraham Ardezoif, John Bandy, Jacob Bixby, Jeremiah Cailot, Thomas Figg, John Gaunt, Evan Gabriel, Thomas Humber, George Hebden, Henry Looker, and John Scarr. In view of the probability that the Grand Secretary, who registered these names in 1751, never saw some of them, written or printed, but simply wrote them from the sound as reported to him, I think this may be considered a very small number.

" So much for " Bro. Norton's classification of the names of the founders of the Antient Grand Lodge.

While on this subject I will call Bro. Norton's attention to another little mistake he has doubtless unintentionally made. It is *not* " Bro. Sadler's theory that the origin of the rival Grand Lodge was due to Pat's revenge for an insult given by the Grand Lodge to three Irish Masons in 1735." The incident mentioned no more represents the complete theory than one stone repre- sents a finished building, which he might easily have seen had he read the whole book with unprejudiced eyes, instead of skimming it over, as he evidently has done, and picking out a bit here and there to suit his present purpose.

My theory is "that the origin of the rival Grand Lodge was due" not to a secession from the Grand Lodge of England, but to a variety of causes duly noted in "Masonic Facts and Fictions," and I say that the affair of 1735 *probably* had something to do with the formation of Irish Lodges in London, which ultimately led to the organization of an independent Society, differing in its system of government, laws and customs, from the body from which it has been supposed to have seceded.

Will Bro. Norton be good enough to give his authority for the following? "Again, of these seventy Grand Lodge makers, no less than seventeen, or about 25 per cent., were soon after *expelled*." This does not quite agree with my reading of the Register, which shows that out of the 78 original members *three* were "expelled" for unworthy conduct, one was "*excluded*' for misbehaviour and not paying his dues," and thirteen were excluded for "non-payment of dues" only, one of whom afterwards "paid his dues and got his certificate." This covers a period ranging from 17th July, 1751, to 25th May, 1754, so that they could not have been so very bad after all, bearing in mind the number of travelling artizans and labourers amongst them. The Grand Lodge Registers of the present day will show that a great many brethren are excluded every year for "non-payment of dues," but it does not follow that they are all men of bad character.

In thus distorting evidence to suit his own views, Bro. Norton evinces plainly his animosity, quite as much so as when he expresses his "firm belief that the remaining 53 of the Antients' originators were not a whit better than those whom they expelled." So far, therefore, from his having proved the worthlessness of the original Antients of 1751, in my opinion he has only proved his inability to discuss this subject with impartiality and strict justice, according to the evidence adduced.

The remainder of the article under examination does not seem to require much attention from me, especially as it in no wise affects the question of Secession ; and with regard to the brief existence of most of the earlier Anglo-Irish Lodges, of which Bro. Norton has furnished evidence, I can only say that I quite agree with him on this point, as it materially strengthens my case ; I beg therefore to thank him most sincerely for having introduced the subject. Had these Lodges been composed of the same class of people as the generality of the Modern Lodges were, viz., shopkeepers, tradesmen, and professional men, permanently residing in London, it is probable that they would have had a more durable foundation and a longer existence ; but as the Register shows them to have been composed chiefly of people whose social standing was somewhat lower, and whose avocations precluded a lengthened residence in any one place, it is not to be wondered at that their first Lodges soon died out.

In Bro. Norton's " Further Comments," of the 9th February, he confesses that he was mistaken in two of his previous aspersions on the character of Laurence Dermott, and he thanks me for having proved that he was wrong.

This is no more than I should have expected from him, and yet it seems but a small reward after having written about twenty-four columns in replying to his attacks. However, I must " be thankful for small mercies ;" but if I am not in error there are several assertions, besides those he has mentioned, which he has failed to substantiate, and which I have proved to have been mistakes, and as he has probably forgotten them, I think it right to refresh his memory by reminding him that he was wrong in saying,

1. " Bro. Sadler never saw a Warrant of the Antients older than 1772."

2. That " Dermott was initiated in Dublin in 1746."

3. That I derived my theory not from the records of Grand Lodge, but from something I had " read here and something there."

N

4. That a certain letter from Ireland was read in Grand Lodge in 1762, whereas it was not read till 1772.

5. That " All the Warrants given by the Antients during the Grand Mastership of the Earl of Blessington have somehow disappeared."

6. The " evidence of Lord Blessington's private installation rests solely on Dermott's testimony."

7. That since the Grand Mastership of the Duke of Montague, the regular Grand Lodge had no difficulty in finding a nobleman who would cheerfully accept the office of Grand Master.

I make no doubt that Bro. Norton will, on reconsideration, readily admit that he was mistaken on these points as well as on the two before mentioned, and should he feel disposed to favour me with a continuation of his " Comments," I shall be extremely obliged if he will give me the benefit of his opinion on certain points referred to in my former replies, more particularly on that of the 12th January, wherein I ask how it is that the brother who was Grand Secretary of the Moderns from 1734 to 1756 did not inform his successor, when telling him all he knew on the subject of the rival Society, that they had originally seceded from the regular Grand Lodge.

I fear that I have severely taxed the patience of my venerable and respected opponent, but he must remember that he gave me plenty to do, and it would have been of no use or advantage whatever had I been content with simply expressing dissent from his views. I had to *prove* that they were wrong, and this I could not do without producing evidence. I trust it will not be deemed *very* presumptuous on my part if I appeal to him to review this matter seriously, calmly, and judiciously, by the light of the evidence I have adduced; to entirely discard the Prestonian spectacles as being worse than useless, tending rather to distort than make clear; but to depend on his own unbiassed judgment and natural goodness of heart; to unite with me in endeavouring to place this portion of our history on a firm and comprehensive basis, easily understood by those who will follow us; and let us sweep away for all time the inappropriate, confusing, and ridiculous appellations which have hitherto been applied to the two great branches of our Order. Let us in future give them their proper titles, neither " Antients," " so-called Antients," " Moderns," " Regulars," " Irregulars," " Schismatics," " Seceders," nor even " Athols," but let us call the elder Society " The Grand Lodge of England," and the younger, say, " The Anglo-Irish Grand Lodge." If my friend can suggest anything better I shall be glad, but in my opinion these designations would be most appropriate. Whether we agree or not on this particular point, I am firmly convinced that sooner or later some such titles will be given them, for the real history of the so-called " Schismatics" has yet to be written ; indeed, I may venture to state that it is now in progress, and that the subject has been taken in hand by one who has both patience and ability to do it full justice, and who, I doubt not, will act upon the maxim that "Historians ought to be precise, truthful, and quite unprejudiced, and neither interest nor fear, hatred nor affection, should cause them to swerve from the path of truth, whose mother is history, the rival of time, the depository of great actions, the witness of what is past, the example and instruction to the present, and the monitor to the future."*

---

* *Cervantes.*—" Masonic Facts and Fictions," page 188.

LODGES NOW IN EXISTENCE
ORIGINALLY FOUNDED
BY
IRISH MASONS IN ENGLAND.

UNFORTUNATELY the earliest returns, or original lists of members, of the Antient Lodges are not now available (probably having been destroyed prior to the Union in 1813) and the Registers seldom contain information as to the former Lodges of the founders or joining members.

The following Applications for Warrants, however, show that, in Constituting Lodges, the Antients recognised no difference between Irish Masons and members of their own jurisdiction.

UNITED INDUSTRIOUS LODGE, No. 31, CANTERBURY.

Antient No. 24. Constituted 24th March, 1806.

A Lodge, No. 24, was Warranted by the Antients at Bristol on the 17th October, 1753, but it only existed about ten years, and the petitioners for the above-named Lodge were given the dormant number.

PETITION AND RECOMMENDATION FOR THE WARRANT

AT CANTERBURY.

" To the Right Worshipfull Deputy Grand Master, Senr. and Junr. Grand Wardens, and the rest of the Grand Officers.

" Right Worshipfull Sirs and Brothers,

We whose names here under written having the Antient Craft at heart, wishing to form ourselves into a body by which we might be enabled to work the Antient Craft according to the Old System as such, must humbly big that you will have the goodness to grant a Warrant by which we might be enabled to make Masons under the aspices of his Grace John Duke of Athol, Grand Master of the Most Antient and Honorable Fraternity of Free and Accepted Masons of England, and should your petitioners' application meet with success they in duty shall be ever bound to pray.

" A list of the Brothers wishing to form themselves into a body :—

George Taylor	of 207 as	W.M.
Thomas Powell	„ 522	S.W.
Duke Buckingham	„ 400	J.W.
Aaron Paris	„ do.	
Jacob Hart	„ do.	
John Spiers	„ do.	
C. Baines	„ do.	
James Crawford	„ 243	

" The Lodge to be holden at the sign of the Marquis of Granby in Canterbury in the County of Kent. Lodge Nights, the second and fourth Saturdays.

" DEAR BR.,

" We the undersigned Officers of Lodge No. 266 Received the Before mention'd petition from Canterbury. By Strict Examination we find them to be Antient Masons, & Likewise worthy to hold a Warrant, We recommend them to you to obtain such. Craving your assistance.

Signed in open Lodge, March 12, 1806.

THO. VINCER, W.M. of L. 266.

JOHN DODD, S.W.

JOSEPH PODEVIN, J.W.

RICHARD EVANS, Secretary."

The petition was also strongly recommended by the Irish Lodge, No. 400.

Six of the eight Founders of this Lodge were undoubtedly Irish Masons. The highest number on the Roll of the Antient Grand Lodge at the time the petition was received was No. 335, Warranted the 18th February 1806. No. 522 under the Irish Constitution was then held in the 4th Regiment, and no doubt this was the Lodge to which the first Senior Warden belonged. Thomas Powell is described in the Recommendatory Letter of No. 400 as a carpenter, and the five petitioners next in rotation were all members of that Lodge, then held in the 13th Light Dragoons, on the Roll of the Grand Lodge of Ireland. Duke Buckingham, the first Junior Warden, is described as Farrier-Major, Royal Horse Artillery; Aaron Paris was a confectioner, Jacob Hart a silversmith, Charles Baines and John Spiers were Quartermasters in the Royal Horse Artillery.

The first Master, George Taylor, is registered as a paviour. His name is not in the Register of No. 207 of the Antients : it is therefore possible that he also may have been on the Irish Register.

James Crawford was an old member of No. 243, Chatham, now No. 184. He was a tailor residing in Canterbury, and was the first Tyler of Lodge No. 24. After the Union of the two Grand Lodges in 1813 this Lodge became No 37 ; on the closing up of the numbers in 1832 it became No. 34 ; and in 1863 it was awarded the number it now bears.

DERWENT LODGE, No. 40, HASTINGS.

Antient No. 36, Constituted 5th April, 1813.

The original No. 36 was Warranted by the Antients at Moorfields, London, 14th August, 1754, but returned no members after 1761. The Petitioners for the above-named Lodge were given the dormant number.

PETITION AND RECOMMENDATION FOR THE WARRANT AT HASTINGS.

"To the Right Worshipful Grand Lodge of Free and Accepted Masons of England, according to the Old Constitutions.

The Petition of several Free and Accepted Masons, according to the Old Constitutions, Shewing that they are regular and registered Master Masons, as will appear by their Private Lodge certificates, which accompanies this Petition :—

That having the extention and prosperity of the Fraternity at heart, your Petitioners are willing to exert their best endeavours to promote and diffuse the genuine principles of Masonry.

That for the convenience of your Petitioners respective dwellings, and other good reasons your Petitioners have agreed to form themselves into a Lodge.

That in consequence of this resolution, your Petitioners humbly pray that a Warrant of Constitution be granted to empower them to assemble for the purposes of Masonry, according to the custom of the Antient Craft.

That the prayer of your Petitioners being granted, they promise strict conformity to all the edicts and commands of the Grand Master, as well as a thorough compliance with all the Laws and Regulations of the Grand Lodge.

In that case they beg leave to nominate, and do recommend Brother Thomas Sargent to be their First Master; Brother Henry Rogers, their Senior Warden; and Brother Thomas Foster, Junior Warden.

To be held at the Cutter Inn, in the Town of Hastings, upon the first Wednesday in the month.

The Petition was signed by the following brethren, five of whom were Irish Masons belonging to No. 62, then held in the Dublin Militia, which Lodge, as will be seen, recommended the Petition :—

Thomas Sargent, of Lodge No. 222, Guernsey,
                                         Master Mariner.
Henry Rogers, of Lodge No. 62, Ireland,
                                         Accomptant.
Thomas Foster, of Lodge No. 62, Ireland,
                                         Draper.
William Catt, of Lodge No. 62, Ireland, Grocer.
William Proud Kent, of Lodge No. 128, London,
                                         Mariner.
Peter M. Powell, of Lodge No. 62, Ireland,
                                         Stationer.
John Bayley, of Lodge No. 62, Ireland,
                                         Accomptant.

Recommendation : We the Master, Wardens, &c., &c., of Lodge No. 62 on the Registry of the Grand Lodge of Ireland, do recommend the within mentioned Petitioners as worthy members of our Antient Fraternity of Free and Accepted Master Masons. That thro' the General Intention of promoting the Craft you will grant them a Warrant.

(Signed)

GEORGE REILLY, Master.

TIMOTHY MEALIA, Senr. Warden.

WILLIAM DAVIS, Junr. Warden.

Hastings, 19th March, 1813."

After the Union of the two Grand Lodges in 1813, this Lodge became No. 54. On the closing up of the numbers in 1832 it became No. 47, and in 1863 it was given the number it now bears.

ATHOL LODGE, No. 74, BIRMINGHAM.

Antient No. 83, Constituted 16th July, 1811.

The original No. 83 was Warranted by the Antients at Stockport, 24th June, 1760. This Lodge returned no members after 1775, and the Warrant was cancelled by Grand Lodge 5th June, 1793, "having neglected to correspond with and refused to pay due respect to this R.W. Grand Lodge."

PETITION FOR THE WARRANT AT BIRMINGHAM.

"To His Grace the Duke of Atholl, Right Worshipful Grand Master, the D.G. Master. &c., &c., of the Grand Lodge of Antient Masons of England, according to the Old Establishment.

The Petition of the undersigned Humbly sheweth, That we have been regularly Admitted Members of the Antient Craft, as will appear by our Grand Lodge Certificates herewith subjoined, but by reason of there being no Lodge in the Town of Birmingham other than the Transient Warrant attached to the Military Body, and having in view the extention of the Royal Craft we humbly solicit you will be pleased to Constitute us into a Lodge and grant us a Warrant for this Laudable purpose.

We do hereby promise our strict obedience to all the Laws, Edicts, and Commands of the Grand Lodge.

In case our Prayer is granted, we beg to nominate

Br. John Thomas to be our First Master, Br. John Nelson to be our Senr Warden, Br. Samuel Hudson our Junr Warden.

Your Petitioners, as in duty bound, will ever Pray."

This Lodge was not only founded by Irish Masons, but was actually constituted by some of the members of No. 305 on the Register of the Grand Lodge of Ireland, held in the 7th Dragoon Guards, a Dispensation having been granted to John Dowling, the Master of that Lodge, to "open and hold a Grand Lodge, and to act as Deputy Grand Master for the space of three hours, and no longer." The Dispensation bears date 16th July, 1811, and is signed by Thomas Harper, Deputy Grand Master. The Lodge was duly constituted, and the first officers installed on the 24th of July, 1811, thirteen brethren (exclusive of the Petitioners) being present on the occasion, all of whom, with one exception, were on the register of Ireland. The names of the Founders were: John Thomas, Master; John Nelson, S.W.; Samuel Hudson, J.W.; William Woods, William Trist, Thomas Page, and Alexander Mills—all members of No. 305, Ireland.

After the Union of the two Grand Lodges in 1813 this Lodge became No. 105, in 1832 it became No. 88, and at the last closing up of the numbers in 1863 it became No. 74.

LODGE OF PERSEVERANCE, No. 155, LIVERPOOL.

Antient No. 204. Constituted at Preston
19th October, 1803.

The original No. 204 was Warranted by the Antients at St. Augustine, Florida, 3rd January, 1778; but if the Lodge was constituted there it probably died out shortly afterwards, as only ten names appear in the Register.

PETITION FOR THE WARRANT AT PRESTON.

"To the Most Noble Prince John, Duke and Marquis of Athol, Master of the Antient Masons, or to his Deputy. The humble petition of James Wright, machine maker; Robert Wright, cotton manufacturer, and James Simpson, cotton manufacturer, all of Preston, in the county of Lancaster,

Sheweth that your petitioners wishes to have an Antient Warrant granted to be held at the house of James Anderson the Legs of Man in Preston aforesaid on the first Monday of every month And if granted will be conformable to the rules and regulations of the Antient Grand Craft and behave themselves in such a manner as the Antient Grand Lodge shall have no occasion to complain

It is requested that if this Warrant be granted that the following persons be named as officers:

James Wright, M., No. 73, under the Constitution of Scotland.

Robert Wright, S.W., No. 333, under the Constitution of Ireland.

James Simpson, J.W., No. 623, under the Constitution of Ireland."

The petition was signed by the Masters and Wardens of the Lodges Nos. 235 Wigan, 238 Chorley, and 310 Blackburn.

No other names appear, either in the Petition or in the Grand Lodge Register, as founders of this Lodge; but nine additional names were returned in January, 1804, some of whom probably assisted in establishing the Lodge.

After the union of the two Grand Lodges in 1813 this Lodge became No. 255, at the closing up of the numbers in 1832 it became No. 181, and in 1863 it became No. 155.

DUKE OF ATHOL LODGE, No. 210, DENTON.

Antient No. 289.   Constituted at Manchester 21st March, 1795.

PETITION FOR THE WARRANT AT MANCHESTER, DATED 24TH FEB., 1795.

To His Grace John Duke, Marquis, Earl of Atholl, &c., &c., Right Worshipful Grand Master, and the rest of the Rt. W. the Grand Officers of the Grand Lodge of Masons, London, according to the Old Institution, &c.

We, whose names are hereunder written and subscribed, being persons residing in the Town of Manchester, in the County of Lancashire, and Regular and Antient Free and Accepted Masons, and duly certified as such under the Certificates and Seal of the Rt. Worshipfull the Grand Lodge of Ireland, and having nothing nearer our hearts than the prosperity of the Craft, do most Humbly request to be Constituted and Installed and formed into a just and perfect Lodge by virtue of a Warrant from and under your Rt. W. Grand Lodge.

That should this our request be granted we promise strict conformity to the edicts and commands of your Rt. W. Grand Lodge, and we beg to Nominate and Recommend Broth⁸ Hugh Ardery to be First Master; James Gillespie, Senʳ· Warden; and Henry Haddock, Junʳ· Warden; and the Lodge to be held at the Royal Archer, Dale Street, Manchester, upon the first Monday of every Callender Month, and, as in duty bound, shall ever pray, &c.

(Signed)   HUGH ARDERY, Intended, Master.
JAMES GILLESPIE,   „   S.W.
HENRY HADDOCK,   „   J.W."

The Petition is recommended and signed by the Masters and Wardens of Nos. 275 and 278, both Antient Lodges meeting in Manchester.

The following are the names of the Founders as they appear in the Petition :—

" Hugh Ardery, first Master, No. 681, muslin manufactorer, on the Regestry of irland.

James Gillespie, muslin weaver, No. 671 on the Regestry of irland.

Henry Haddock, muslin weaver, No. 393 on the Regestry of irland.

John Honey, muslin weaver, No. 333 on the Regestry of irland.

George McCormick, muslin weaver, No. 715 on the Regestry of irland.

Andrew Hunter, muslin weaver, No. 333 on the Regestry of irland.

Hugh Holmes, muslin weaver, No. 459 on the Regestry of irland.

Robert Hamilton, muslin weaver, No. 460 on the Regestry of irland.

John Morgan, muslin weaver, No. 618 on the Regestry of irland.

John Park, muslin weaver, No. 741 on the Regestry of irland.

James Irwin, muslin weaver, No. 404 on the Regestry of irland.

Daniel Doras, Tailor, No. 715 on the Regestry of irland.

John Parker, muslin weaver, No. 526 on the Regestry of irland.

James Coal, muslin weaver, No. 592 on the Regestry of irland.

Robert Carrol, muslin weaver, No. 673 on the Regestry of irland,

William Sedgwick, muslin manufacturer, No. 716 on the Regestry of irland.

Moses Halmond, muslin weaver, No. 465 on the Regestry of irland.

Robert Lister, muslin weaver, No. 184 on the Regestry of irland.

Moses Mitchell, muslin weaver, No 450 on the Regestry of irland."

To my thinking, no great stretch of imagination is required to be able to arrive at the conclusion that what was done in 1795 might just as easily have been done at an earlier period, and that prior to the organization of the Antient or Anglo-Irish Grand Lodge these Irish Masons assembled and worked without Warrants, or any other authority, as they themselves admit in their early records, and, indeed, as all other Masons did before the institution of Grand Lodges.

This Lodge became No. 366 after the Union in 1813, at the closing up of the numbers in 1832 it became No. 254, and in 1863 it became No. 210.

EUPHRATES LODGE, No. 212, LONDON.

Antient No. 292. Constituted at Greenwich 16th October, 1812.

The original No. 292 was constituted at Stockport, 20th Nov., 1795, but the Lodge died out about 10 years later, and the Warrant was subsequently transferred to Greenwich.

PETITION FOR THE WARRANT AT STOCKPORT, DATED OCTOBER 26TH, 1795.

" Right Worshipfull Sir and Brother

We the Masters, Wardens, Past Masters and Brethren of Lodges No. 268 and No. 279 at Stockport in the County of Chester request thro' you to supplicate the

Antient Grand Lodge of England and lay before them the application of our Brothers Thomas Shaw of Lodge No. 491, Joiner and Turner; James Rea of Lodge No. 395, Taylor; and John Field of Lodge No. 760, Muslin Weaver, all of the Kingdom of Ireland, being Master Masons, and whom we strongly recommend as worthy Brothers and supplicate the Grand Lodge to grant them a Warrant for holding a Lodge and making Free Masons according to Antient Custom at Thomas Grundy's, the Fleece Tavern in Chestergate in Stockport aforesaid, the title of the Lodge to be call'd the Royal Arch Lodge of St. John of Jerusalem, and their regular meeting nights to be the Monday after every full moon.   And we do hereby recommend our said Brother Thomas Shaw to be the first Master of the new Lodge, James Rea to be his Senior Warden, and John Field to be his Junior Warden, being every way properly qualified for the said offices. And we firmly believe that when our said Brothers are duly Constituted and form'd into a Regular Lodge, they will strictly conform to the Laws and Regulations of Masonry, &c., &c."

Signed by the Masters, Wardens, and Past Masters of Nos. 268 and 279.

Addressed to Robert Leslie, Grand Secretary.

After the Union of the two Grand Lodges in 1813 this Lodge became No. 370, at the closing up of the numbers in 1832 it became No. 257, and in 1863 it became No. 212.

PROVINCIAL GRAND MASTERS

APPOINTED BY, OR EMANATING FROM,

THE ANTIENT GRAND LODGE.

A DISTINCT difference may be observed between the Moderns and the Antients in the mode of appointing Provincial Grand Masters. By the former, such appointments, being considered the personal prerogative of the Grand Master for the time being, were seldom even reported to the Grand Lodge after the first few years of its existence. Hence nearly every county in England and Wales, as well as many of the colonial districts and several foreign countries, had a Provincial Grand Master, although in some few instances the head of the province had no lodges to rule over.

A complete list of the Provincial Grand Masters under the Modern Grand Lodge will be found in the Grand Lodge Calendar, but no attempt has hitherto been made to collate those of the Antients, who allowed their Grand Masters no such privilege as before mentioned, the appointments being very few, and only made in response to petitions to the Grand Lodge.

When a new lodge was to be opened, either at home or abroad, it was customary for the authorities to issue a Dispensation to some duly-qualified brother in the neighbourhood to act as Deputy Grand Master *pro tem*, and to "open and hold a Grand Lodge, for the space of three hours only," for the purpose of Constituting the lodge and Installing the first officers.

So far as I can learn, the appointment of a Provincial Grand Master for York, Chester, and Lancaster was the only one made in England.

The brethren abroad, after a Provincial Grand Warrant had been granted and a person nominated as first Provincial Grand Master, seldom troubled the

O

home authorities for a successor, but selected one for themselves, and merely reported the name to the Grand Secretary when they sent him a list of their officers ; and as that functionary kept no record of such appointments this list may not be absolutely perfect in every particular.

These Provincial Grand Lodges were Warranted and given a number on the general list of lodges, in most cases taking a local number as well.

The names are arranged as nearly as possible in chronological order according to seniority or the date of the appointment of the first Provincial Grand Master.

NOVA SCOTIA.

1757	Major ERASMUS JAMES PHILIPS.
1784	JOHN GEORGE PYKE, Esq.
1786	His Excellency JOHN PARR.
1791–1800	Hon. RICHARD BULKELEY.
1800–1	DUNCAN CLARK, Esq.
1802–10	His Excellency Sir JOHN WENTWORTH, Bart.
1810–20	JOHN GEORGE PYKE, Esq. (*Past G. Master*)

PENNSYLVANIA.

1761   WILLIAM BALL, Esq.

Grand Lodge Minutes, 2nd December, 1772 :

"D.G. Master Dermott laid before this Lodge a certain manuscript attested by Br. John Wood, G. S. in Philadelphia as the Transactions of the Provincial Grand Lodge of Pennsylvania, commencing on the 30th day of December, 1763, and continued to the 30th April, 1772.

"Unanimously Agreed and Ordered that a Committee consisting of the Grand Officers should take the said Transactions, &c., into their serious consideration, and that their judgment upon the whole should be Decisive and final.

"*Ibid.*, 15th December, 1773.

"Heard the Answer sent to the Provincial Grand Lodge of Pennsylvania to their Transactions, which was unanimously approved of."

MONTSERRAT AND NEVIS.

1767   Dr. THOMAS FOGARTY.

MINORCA.

1772   ALEXANDER MERCER.

MADRAS.

1778   Three members of No. 152, at Fort St. George, were appointed by the Antient Grand Lodge as a Provincial Grand Committee, with power to grant Dispensations for new Lodges, &c.

1781   JOHN SYKES, Esq.

YORK, CHESTER. AND LANCASTER.

1781   HUGH CHENEY, Esq

NEW YORK.

1781   Rev. WILLIAM WALTER, M.A.

ANDALUSIA, OR GIBRALTAR.

1786   A Provincial Grand Lodge (No. 220) was Warranted at Gibraltar Jan. 25, 1786.

> [A Provincial Grand Master is not then mentioned; but one appears to have been elected annually after 1791, prior to which year no returns or records are now available.]

O 1

1791   Lieut.-Col. JOHN BRIDGES SCHAW, 68th Regt.*
1792   SAMUEL SALTER, Quarter-Master 11th Regt.
1793   ABRAHAM S. WILLCOX, Quarter-Mr. 32nd Regt.
1794-96   JOHN VINCENT, Esq., Master of Royal Armoury.
1797   Hon. Capt. RAMSEY, 100th Regt.
1799   WILLIAM TRAVERS, Quarter-Master 48th Regt.
1802-3   THOMAS DODDS, Captain Royal Artillery.
1803-4   JOHN BROWN, Sergt. Royal Military Artificers.
1804-5   HAMILTON FINNEY, Quarter-Master 54th Regt.
1806   CHARLES NELSON, Sergt. Royal Artillery.
1807   W. R. RORK.
1808   JOHN WINTERS.
1811   WILLIAM MASON.

CANADA (LOWER).

1792-1812 H.R.H. PRINCE EDWARD, Duke of Kent.
1812-22   Hon. CLAUDE DENECHAU.

CANADA (UPPER).

1792   WILLIAM JARVIS, Esq.
1804   GEORGE FORSYTH, Esq.   } Elected. *
1807-11   Hon. ROBERT KERR, Esq.   }

> [Wm. Jarvis evidently neglected his Provincial duties.
> The two last-named being schismatic appoint-
> ments, were not officially acknowledged by the
> Antient Grand Lodge.]

JAMAICA.

1796   Hon. WILLIAM BLAKE.
1797   Col. WILLIAM VICK.
1809   MOSES BELISARIO.
1811   FRANCIS OWEN, Esq.

---

* *These brethren may have been elected earlier.*

OFFICERS OF THE GRAND LODGE

OF

THE ANTIENTS, FROM 1752 TO 1813,

WITH THE NUMBERS OF THEIR LODGES.

N O attempt has hitherto been made to collate and print a complete list of the Grand Officers of the Antients. Those of the Moderns will be found in their Grand Lodge Calendar from 1775 to 1814.

The figures on the right of the names denote the Number of the lodge on the Antient register prior to the Union in 1813.

Lane's Masonic Records, 1895, contains the numbers since borne by the same lodges if still in existence.

GRAND MASTERS.*

		No.
1753-54	Robert Turner	15
1755-56	Hon. Edward Vaughan	4
1756-60	Earl of Blesinton; (as Viscount Mountjoy) G.M. Ireland, 1738 and 1739	1
1760-66	Thomas, Earl of Kelly	1
1766-70	Hon. Thomas Mathew, Prov. G.M. of Munster	1
1771-74	John, 3rd Duke of Atholl, G.M. of Scotland. 1773. Died 1774	1

		No.
1775-81	John, 4th Duke of Atholl, G.M. of Scotland, 1778-79	1
1782	Vacant.†	
1783-91	Randal, Earl of Antrim, afterwards Marquess of Antrim, G.M. of Ireland, 1773 and 1779.	
1791-1813	John, 4th Duke of Atholl	1
1813	H.R.H. the Duke of Kent	

----

* From about 1751 to 1753 this Body was governed by a Grand Committee.

† During this year William Dickey, late D.G.M., exercised the authority of G.M., as President of the Grand Committee.

DEPUTY GRAND MASTERS.

		No.				No.
1753-54	William Rankin	15	1771-77	Laurence Dermott	...	5
1754-55	William Holford	21	1777-81	William Dickey*	...	37
1755-56	William Rankin		1783-87	Laurence Dermott	...	5
1756-58	William Holford		1787-90	James Perry ...	...	81
1758-59	Robert Goodman	15	1790-94	James Agar ...	...	81
1759-64	William Osborne	6	1794-1800	William Dickey	...	6
1764-71	William Dickey	6	1801 13	Thomas Harper	...	1

GRAND WARDENS.

		No.			No.
1753-54	Samuel Quay, S.G.W.	2	1764 William Dickey, S.G.W.	37
„ „	Lachlan MacIntosh, J.G.W. ...	3	„ James Gibson, J.G.W....	5
1754	JohnAbercromby,J.G.W.†	15	1765 James Gibson, S.G.W....	5
1755	John Jackson, S.G.W....	10	„ John Howell, J.G.W. ..	49
„	Samuel Galbraith,J.G.W.	3	„ Richard Swan, J.G.W.§	14
1756	JohnAbercromby,S.G.W.	15	1766 James Gibson, S.G.W....	5
„	James Nisbett. J.G.W....	21	„ Richard Swan, J.G.W....	14
1757	Capt. Jas. Nisbett, S.G.W.	21	1767 William Clarke, S.G.W.	81
„	JohnAbercromby,J.G.W.	15	„ Peter Duffy, J.G.W. ...	31
1758	Robert Goodman, S.G.W.	15	1768 Hon. Edmund Butler S.G.W.	—
„	William Osborne, J.G.W.	37	„ Henry Allen, J.G.W. ...	—
1759	William Osborne, S.G.W.	37	1769-72 William Clarke,S.G.W.	81
„	David Fisher, J.G.W. ..	48	„ „ Jno. Christian,J.G.W.	14
1760-62	David Fisher. S.G.W.‡	48	1773-74 Jno. Christian,S.G.W.	14
„ „	William Dickey,J.G.W.	37	„ „ Peter Shatwell,J.G.W.	14
1763	William Dickey, S.G.W.	37	1775-76 Wm Tindall, S.G.W.	9
„	Daniel Garnault, J.G.W.	81	„ „ Thomas Carter,J.G.W.	5

* No Grand Master elected from December, 1781, to September, 1782, consequently no Dep. G. Master was appointed.

† Elected for the latter half of 1754.

‡ "David Fisher. late Grand Warden Elect, having attempted to form a Grand Lodge of his own, and offered to Register Masons therein for sixpence each, was deem'd unworthy of any office or seat in the Grand Lodge."—*G.L. Minutes*, 27th December, 1762.

§ Elected for the latter half of 1765.

		No				No.
1777	Thomas Carter, S.G.W.	5	1796	Joseph Brown, J.G.W.		1
„	Robert Davy, J.G.W.	14	1797	Joseph Brown, S.G.W.		1
1778-79	Robert Davy, S.G.W.	14	„	George Bowen, J.G.W.		3
„ „	George Stewart, J.G.W.	14	1798	Robert Gill, S.G.W.		5
1780	George Stewart, S.G.W.	14	„	George Bowen. J.G.W.		3
„	James Jones, J.G.W.	205	1799	Robert Gill. S.G.W.		5
1781	James Jones, S.G.W.	205	„	Thos. Hanscomb, J.G.W.		240
„	James Read, J.G.W.	5	1800-1	Robert Gill, S.G.W.		5
1782-83	James Read, S.G.W.	5	„ „	William Burwood, J.G.W.		23
„ „	Robert Leslie, J.G.W.	5	1802	Wm. Burwood, S.G.W.		23
1783	William Dagnia, J.G.W.*	4	„	William Chaplin, J.G.W.		195
1784	James Read, S.G.W.	5	1803	William Chaplin, S.G.W.		195
„	Peter Fehr. J.G.W.	194	„	John Betts, J.G.W.		7
1785	Peter Fehr, S.G.W.	194	1804	William Chaplin, S.G.W.		195
„	Benjamin Good, J.G.W.	2	„	Chas. Humphreys, J.G.W.		225
„	John Feakins, J.G.W.†	6	1805	Chas. Humphreys, S.G.W.		225
1786	John Feakins, S.G.W.	6	„	Ben. Plummer, J.G.W.		10
„	Thomas Harper, J.G.W.	5	1806	Ben. Plummer, S.G.W.		10
1787	Thomas Harper, S.G.W.	5	„	John Bryant Roach, J.G W.		244
„	James Perry, J.G.W.	81	1807	John Bryant Roach, S.G.W		244
1788-89	Thos. Harper, S.G.W.	5	„	Rd. Humphreys, J.G.W.		225
„ „	James Agar, J.G.W.	81	1808	Rd. Humphreys, S.G.W.		225
1790	James Agar, S.G.W.	81	„	Thomas Scott, J.G.W.		1
„	Sir Watkin Lewes, M.P., J.G.W.	1	1809	Thomas Scott, S.G.W.		1
			„	Malcolm Gillies, J.G.W.		1
1791-92	Sir Watkin Lewes, M.P., S.G.W.	1	1810	Malcolm Gillies, S.G.W.		1
„ „	John Bunn, J.G.W.	1	„	Thomas Mahon, J.G.W.		8
1793	John Bunn, S.G.W	1	1811	Thomas Mahon, S.G.W.		8
„	William A. Howard, M.D., J.G.W.	1	„	William Oaks, J.G.W.		255
1794	John Bunn, S.G.W.	1	1812	William Oaks, S.G.W.		255
„	Wm. Hockaday, J.G.W.	193	„	Archibald Herron, J.G.W.		8
1795	John Bunn, S.G.W.	1	1813	Archibald Herron, S.G.W.		8
„	Robert Gill, J.G.W.	5	„	Jeremiah Cranfield, J.G W.		255
1796	Robert Gill, S.G.W.	5				

* From March 6th. Leslie appointed Grand Secretary.
† The latter half of 1785.

GRAND SECRETARIES

		No.			No.
1751-2	John Morgan ...	2	1783-85	Robert Leslie ...	5
1752-71	Laurence Dermott	10	1785-90	John McCormick	6
1771-77	William Dickey ..	37	1790-1813	Robert Leslie .. }	5
1777-79	James Jones ..	205	1792-95	Thomas Harper... }	1
1779-83	Charles Bearblock	4			

DEPUTY GRAND SECRETARIES.

		No.			No.
1768	William Dickey, Jun.	14	1797-1800	Thomas Harper ...	1
			1801-13	Edwards Harper	1

GRAND TREASURERS.*

		No.			No.
1764-69	Matthew Beath ...	81	1775-80	John Ryland ...	14
1769-70	John Starkey ...	2	1780-86	Robert Galloway	205
1770-73	Thomas Smith ...	14	1786-98	John Feakins ...	6
1773	John Peck... ...	14	1798-1813	Wm. Comerford Clarkson ...	1
	(Only served six months.)				
1773-75	William Clarke ..	81			

GRAND CHAPLAINS.†

		No.			No.
1772-75	Rev. James Grant, LL.D.	3	1786-91	Rev. Dr. Colin Milne, F.R.S.	1
1775-78	Rev. Parker Rowlands		1791-1813	Rev. Edward Barry, A.M., M.D.	1
1779-82	Rev. Dr. William Parry	14			

DEPUTY GRAND CHAPLAIN.

1809-13 Rev. Henry John Knapp.

---

* Prior to 1764 no Grand Treasurer was elected, the Grand Officers taking charge of the cash, which was kept in the Lodge Chest.

† For several years prior to the appointment of a Grand Chaplain Bros. Parker Rowlands, and James Grant had preached to the brethren on St. John's Day in Midsummer.

GRAND SWORD BEARERS.*

		No.				No.
1788-93	William Hockaday	193	1806	Rich. Humphreys	..	225
1793-94	Robert Gill ...	5	1807	Thomas Scott...	..	1
1794-98	Thomas Hanscomb	240	1808	Malcolm Gillies	..	1
1798-1800	Chas. Hockstetter	5	1809	Thomas Mahon	...	8
1800-1801	Andrew Barry ...	243	1810	William Oaks...	..	255
1802	John Betts	7	1811	Archibald Herron ...		8
1803	Chas. Humphreys ...	225	1812	Jeremiah Cranfield	..	255
1804	Benjamin Plummer	10	1813	Robert McCann	..	244
1805	Robert Barry ..	.. 5				

GRAND PURSUIVANTS.

		No.			No.
1762-56	William Lilly	... 2	1777-80	James Irwin ...	3
1756-63	Richard Gough	...	1781-91	Henry Westley ...	6
1764-65	David Lyon	.. 15	1791-1813	Benjamin Aldhouse	63
1765-77	Joseph Martin	.. 32			

GRAND TYLERS.

		No.			No.
1752-56	Richard Gough	...	1765-77	Nathaniel England	
1756-57	— Jones ...	...	1777-82	Peter Biddleux ...	63
1758-60	Joseph Webb	... 3	1782-91	Benjamin Aldhouse	63
1760-63	David Lyon	... 15	1791-1803	James Swan ..	8
1764-65	Joseph Martin	32	1803-13	James Marler ..	81

* Grand Lodge Minutes June 3rd, 1772.
" Agreed that a Brother be appointed pro-tempore to carry the Sword at Public Processions, and that Bro. Nash, Master of No. 2, carry the same next St. John's Day."
No further mention of the Sword Bearer appears in the Minutes until 1788.

INDEX.

Subscribers' Names.

A

ABBOTT, GEORGE BLIZARD, P.M. No. 1385, Past Prov. G. Deacon, Herts.

ABRAHAM, S. V., Past G. Pursuivant, England.

ABRAHAM, Dr. P. S., W.M. No. 2620.

ADAMS, FRANK, P.M. No. 1259.

ADAMS, HERBERT J., Past G. Sword Bearer, England.

ADAMS, JAMES, No. 2148.

ALDRICH, A. G., M.D., No. 30, Minnesota.

ALLSOP, THOMAS W., P.M. Nos. 88, 2492.

AMHERST, EARL, Prov. G. Master, Kent, and Deputy G. Master of England.

AMHERST OF HACKNEY, LORD, Past G. Warden, England.   (2 copies.)

ARMITAGE, EDWARD, P.M. Nos. 859, 1074, P.P.S.G.W. Cumberland and Westmoreland.

ARMITAGE, WILLIAM J., No. 859.

ARMSTRONG, JOHN, P.M., Nos. 148, 1250, 1350, 2433, 2651, P.P.G.W. Cheshire

ASHWELL, T. S. H., P.M. No. 1391, P.P.G.S. Bearer.

ATKINS, HENRY J., P.P.S.G. Warden, Norths and Hunts.

ATKINSON, P. L., No. 2547.

B

BADDELEY, WILLIAM, W.M. No. 25, 1385, Prov. G. Steward, Herts.

BAIN, GEORGE WASHINGTON, P.M. No. 949, P.P.G. Registrar, Durham.

BAKER, FRANK, P.M. No. 31.

BARFIELD, ASHER, Past G. Treasurer, England.

BARNARD, G. W. G., P.M. No. 943, Prov. G. Secretary, Norfolk.

BARNES, CHARLES B., P.M., Secretary No. 19.

P

BARRON, E. JACKSON, Past G. Deacon, England.

BARRY, CHARLES, Past G. Superintendent of Works, England.

BARTHOLOMEW, GILBERT, P.M. Nos. 29, 1260, 1673.

BAYNE, RICHARD C., I.P.M. No. 1044.

BEALE, ARTHUR G., P.M., Treasurer No. 59.

BELL, SEYMOUR, P.S.G. Warden, Northumberland.

BENNETT, ALFRED B., P.P.S.G. Deacon, East Lancashire.

BETTS, ARTHUR, P.M. No. 1351.

BEYNON, J. H., Assistant Secretary No. 2657.

BILLINGHURST, W. B., P.M. No. 822.   (2 copies).

BISHOP, HENRY, P.M. No. 632, P.P.G.S. Bearer, Wilts.

BIXBY, CHARLES, P.M. No. 24, Kansas.

BLANCHETTE, WALTER E., No. 2427.

BLYTON, FRED. W., P.M. and Treasurer, No. 2148.

BOULTON, JAMES, P.M. Nos. 28, 1056, &c., &c., Past G. Pursuivant, England.

BOWLES, Col. FRED. A., R.A., P.D.D.G. Master, Punjab, &c.

BOWSER, WILFRID A., W.M. No. 2000.

BOYLES, HENRY R., No. 30.

BRADSHAW, ROBERT, P.M. No. 854, Ireland.

BREWER, CHARLES S., W.M. No. 2433.

BRIGGS, WILLIAM, W.M. No. 45.

BRISCOE, J. POTTER, *F.R.H.S.*, No. 47, Prov. G Librarian, Notts.

BROOKE, HENRY W., Steward No. 21.

BROOKS, FRANCIS A., M.D., S.D. No. 2371.

BROOKS, W. E.

BROWN, WILLIAM PETER, Past G. Standard Bearer, England.   (2 copies.)

BROWN, R. S., G.S.E. Scotland.   (2 copies.)

BROWN, JULIUS L., No. 96, Georgia.

BROWNRIGG, Rev. J. S., Past G. Chaplain, England.

BRUCE, ALEX., Nos. 85, 772, Scotland.

BURNAND, A. A., P.M. No. 51, Colorado.

BURNE, THOMAS, P.M. No. 162, P.P.S.G. Deacon, Surrey.

BURTCHAELL, G. D., J.W. No. 357, 241, &c., Ireland.

BYARD, HENRY T., P.M. No. 1347, P.P.G.D.C. Surrey.

BYRNE, JOHN, P.M. No. 89 (I.C.), Grand Inspector, Antrim.

BYWATER, WITHAM M., Past G. Sword Bearer, England.

C

CALVERT, ALBERT F., W.M. No. 28.

CARSON, JOE L., P.M., Prov. J.G. Deacon, Tyrone and Fermanagh.

CARTEIGHE, MICHAEL, P.M. No. 2394.

CASE, ROBERT, Prov. G. Sec., Dorset, Past G. Sword Bearer, England.

CHAPIN, A. C., P.M. No. 137, Prov. A.G.D.C. Dorset.

CHAPMAN, ARTHUR W., P.M. Nos. 289, 2397.

CLARK, GEORGE W. O. F., P.M. No. 86 (I.C.), P.P.S.G. Warden, Down.

CLAYSON, JAMES, P.M. No. 360, P.P.J.G. Warden, Norths and Hunts.

CLEAVE, J. R., P.P.G. Deacon, Surrey.

COCK, Dr. WILLIAMS, P.M. No. 1597, 2024, 2272, P.P.S.G. Deacon, Middlesex.

COHU, THOMAS, P.M. No. 192, P.P.G.W. Guernsey and Alderney.

COLLINS, FRED. J., W.M. No. 74.

COLLINS, HOWARD J., W.M. No. 587, 887.

COLLINS, JOSIAH, P.M. No. 74, P.P.G. Deacon, Warwickshire.

COMLEY, THOMAS J., No. 2547.

COOKE, J. STONEMAN, No. 2271.

COOKSON, JAMES, P.M., Sec. No. 287, P.P.G. Treas. Cheshire.

COOMBS, ROWLAND H., M.D., P.G.D.C. Beds.

CORNFORD, HENRY, S.W. No. 1922.

CORRIE, ALEXANDER, P.D.S.G. Warden, Queensland.

COULTER, JAMES, P.M. No. 21. Ireland.

CRABTREE, CHARLES, P.P.G. Deacon, W. Yorkshire.

CRAVEN, JOHN E., P.P.G. Reg. W. Yorkshire.

CRAWLEY, W. J. CHETWODE, LL.D., D.C.L., Senior G. Deacon, Ireland

CREED, RICHARD, P.M. No. 1, Past G. Steward, England.

CROWE, FREDERICK J.W., W.M. No. 328, P.P.G. Org. Devon.

CRUTCH, W. J., P.P.G. Deacon, Herts.

D

DANDRIDGE, ALFRED C., P.M. No. 871.

DANIELS, L. E., No. 826, Illinois.

DARELL, Sir LIONEL EDWARD, Bart., Past G. Deacon, England.

DAVIES, THOMAS EDWARD, P.M. No. 1950.

DAVY, WILLIAM NORMAN, No. 1385.

DAY, J. G., P.M., Sec. No. 703, Ireland.

P I

DEATS, HIRAM E., P.M. No. 37, New Jersey.

DE FERRIERES, Baron. Past G. Deacon, England.

DEHANE, H. E., P.P.S.G. Deacon, Essex.

DERBYSHIRE, J. S., No. 1045, S.D. 1567.

DEWSBURY, ALFRED, P.M., P.P.G.D.C. Staffordshire.

DIMSDALE, JOHN, I.G. No. 1, J.D. No. 31.

DIPROSE, JOHN, P.M., Treasurer No. 957.

DIPROSE, HENRY L., P.M. No. 1853.

DODD, WILLIAM. P.M. No. 1194, P.P.G.D. Middlesex.

DONOUGHMORE, The Earl of, K.C.M.G., Past S.G. Warden, England.

DOWNIE, WILLIAM, Past G. Master, British Columbia.

DUCK, G. W., Steward No. 1687.

DUKAS, N., S.D. No. 2398.

DURET, ARMAND W., P.M. Nos. 1223, 1763, W.M. No. 1491, P.P.S.G.D. Kent.

E

EAST, SAMUEL A., S.W. No. 2148.

EDGLEY, R. W., P.M. (Late No. 1446).

EDWARDS, CHARLES L. FRY, Senior G. Deacon, England.

EDYVEAN, BERNARD F., A.G.D. of Ceremonies, England.

ELLARD, GEORGE, P.M., P.P.G.S. Warden, Prov. G.D. of Ceremonies, Norths and Hunts.

ENNIS, JOSEPH, W.M. No. 500, Ireland.

EVENDEN, HENRY, P.M. No. 749.

EWART, CHARLES, No. 1118.

F

FENN, THOMAS, Past G. Warden, England.   (12 copies).

FIELD, JAMES, No. 144.

FLORENCE, HENRY L., G. Supt. Works, England.

FOX-THOMAS, Rev. E., P.M. No. 312, P.P.G. Chaplain, N. and E. Yorks.

FOXTON, WILLIAM. No. 19.

FRANCIS, THOMAS, P.M., P.P.G. Warden, Hants and I. of Wight.

FRANCIS, CHARLES K., P.M. No. 610, Philadelphia.

FROST, FRED. C., *F.S.I.*, P.P.G. Supt. of Works, Devon.

FULFORD, FREDERICK H., Nos. 68 and 610.

G

GADD, H. JOHN, S.W. No. 1067.

GALE, JOHN, P.M. No. 1965.

GARDINER, THOMAS HENRY, P.A.G.D. Ceremonies, England.

GARDNER, GEORGE M., No. 339, Canada.

GILBERT, JOHN, Prov. G. Tyler Middlesex.

GILES, H. G., P.M. No. 1903, P.P.G. Registrar, Hants and Isle of Wight.

GOAD, WILLIAM, No. 1571.

GODSON, Dr. CLEMENT, Past G. Deacon, England.

GOODACRE, WILLIAM, Prov. G. Secretary, W. Lancashire, Past G. Sword Bearer, England. (2 copies.)

GOODALL, JOHN F., W.M. No. 1271.

GOULD, ROBERT F., Past G. Deacon, England.

GOWAN, CHARLES, P.M., Secretary No. 1989, P.P.G. Warden, Cumberland and Westmoreland.

GOWAN, ROBERT A., P.M. No. 2029, Nos. 1 and 133, Scotland.

GRAND LODGE LIBRARY, England. (2 copies.)

GRAND LODGE LIBRARY, IOWA.

GRAND LODGE LIBRARY, Massachusetts.

GRAND LODGE LIBRARY, Mark Master Masons.

GRAVELEY, GEORGE, Grand Pursuivant, England. (2 copies.)

GREEN, ABRAHAM, Past G. Pursuivant, England.

GREY, ROBERT, Past G. Warden, England.

GRIGGS, ROBERT, P.M. No. 228.

GRIST, RALPH COULTHARD, No. 2523.

H

HARDING, JAMES W., P.M. No. 1585.

HARDING, WILLIAM, No. 632.

HARE, SHOLTO HENRY, P.M., P.P.G. Deacon, Cornwall. (3 copies.)

HARRIS, SIR GEORGE DAVID, Past S.G. Deacon, England.

HARRISON, GEORGE, No. 1326.

HARRISON, WILLIAM, P.M. No. 265.

HAYES, SIMEON, P.P.S.G. Warden, West Yorkshire

HAYWARD, M. CECIL, No. 859.

HEAP, HERBERT R., P.M. No. 1369, P.P.G. Deacon, N. Wales

HEDGES, FRANCIS R. W., Past G. Sword Bearer, England, Secretary R.M.I. Girls.

HEMING, G. BOOTH, P.M., Secretary No. 256.

HIGERTY, ALEX. C. A., W.M. No. 2697, P.P.G.W., Berks. (2 copies.)

HOARE, CHARLES H., No. 1629.

HOBBISS, W. H., P.M. No. 858.

HODGES, SYDNEY, No. 2030.

HODGKINSON, JOHN N., Tyler Ferdinand de Rothschild Lodge, No. 2420.

HOIT. JOHN HENRY. P.M. No. 856. P.P.G.S.B. Cornwall.

HOPE, ANDREW, P.M. No. 39.

HOTME, JOHN, No. 1950.

HUDSON, ROBERT, Prov. G. Sec. Durham, Past G. Sword Bearer, England.

HUGHAN, WILLIAM JAMES, P.M. No. 131, Past S.G. Deacon, England.

HUNT, CHARLES P.M., Secretary No. 194.

HUNT, Dr. DE VERE, Nos. 348, 2547.

HURFORD, WILLIAM, No. 960.

HUTCHINSON, THOMAS, S.W. No. 1900.

HUTCHINSON, THOMAS OWEN, Steward No. 1900.

I

INGRAM, THOMAS, No. 473. Ireland.

IVEY. F. G., W.M. No. 99, P.M. No. 231, Past G. Steward, England.

J

JAQUES, W., M.D., Past Dist. Dep. G. Master, Canada.

JENKINSON, Capt. H. L. A., P.M. No. 1789.

JONES, THOMAS, Past G. Deacon, England.

K

KELL, CHARLES F., (late No. 2148).

KEMPSTER, W. H., M.D., P.M., Past G. Steward, England.

KENNING, GEORGE, P.M., Nos. 192, 1657, Past P.G. Deacon, Middlesex.

KENNING, FRANK REGINALD, No. 192.

KENT, GEORGE C., P.A.G.D. Ceremonies, England.

KENTISH, WILLIAM GEORGE. Past G. Stand. Bearer, England (2 copies.)

KILPIN, S. L., P.M. No. 540.

KING-EDWARDS, E., J.P., D.L., P.M. No. 199, Ireland.

KLEIN, SYDNEY T., F.L.S., F.R.A.S., W.M. No. 2076.

KNIGHTLEY, Capt. C. J., P.M. No. 1745.

KUPFERSCHMIDT, C., Asst. G. Sec. German Correspondence, England.

KYNASTON, Rev. Canon, D.D., Past G. Chaplain, England.

L

LAKE, WILLIAM, Assistant Grand Secretary, England.

LAMB, H. T., No. 1185. (3 copies.)

LAMBERT, Col. GEORGE, Past G. Sword Bearer, England.

LAMBERTON, J. M., P.M. No. 21, Pennsylvania.

LAMONBY, WILLIAM F., Past Dep. Grand Master, Victoria.

LANCASTER, JOHN, P.M., Secretary, No. 534.

LANE, CHARLES S., P.P.S.G. Warden, Durham. (2 copies.)

LANE, JOHN, F.C.A., Past Assist. G.D. Ceremonies, England.

LANE, W. H., P.M. No. 232, D.C. Grand Lodge of Instruction, Ireland.

LANGTON, J. D., Past Dep. G.D. Ceremonies, England.

LARDNER, HENRY J., P.M. No. 60, Past G. Steward, England.

LAST, JOHN T., P.M. & Sec. No. 2321, P.P.G. Reg., W. Yorks

LAWRENCE, General SAMUEL C., Past G. Master, Massachusetts.

LAZARUS, LEWIS, P.M., Sec. No. 188, Assist. G. Pursuivant, England.

LAZARUS, EMANUEL, S.W. No. 2313.

LAZARUS, HENRY, P.M. and W.M. No. 188.

LE FEUVRE, Major J. E., Past D.P.G.M. Hants and Isle of Wight, Past G. Deacon, England.

LENA, JOSEPH, No. 11. (2 copies.)

LE STRANGE, HAMON, Past. G. Deacon England, Prov. G. Master, Norfolk.

LETCHWORTH, EDWARD, F.S.A., Grand Secretary, England. (2 copies.)

LETTS, ALFRED W., No. 2509.

LIBRARY, Carnarvon Lodge, No. 804.

LIBRARY, MASONIC, Prov. G. Lodge, West Yorkshire.

LODGE, LOYAL BLUE, No. 119, Ireland.

LODGE, MOUNT EVEREST, No. 2439.

LODGE, UNITY, No. 238, Dublin. (2 copies.)

LODGE, QUATUOR CORONATI, No. 2076.

LODGE, WITHAM, No. 297, Lincoln.

LOEWY, BENNO, Local Secretary, New York, Quatuor Coronati Lodge.

LONG, PETER DE LANDE, Past G. Deacon, England.

LONGMAN, H., P.P.G. Supt. of Works, West Lancashire.

LONGSTREET, ALBERT, I.G. No. 1271.

LONGWORTH, ROWLAND D., P.M. No. 1816.'

LUCKING, ALBERT, Past G. Pursuivant, England.

LUSTY, JOHN, P.M. No. 1259.   (2 copies.)

M

MACGREGOR, JAMES, No. 2148.

MACGREGOR, BENJAMIN F. G., No. 2148.

MACINTOSH, JAMES. P.M. No. 59.

McINTYRE, JOHN, No. 232, Dublin.

McKIRDY, HUGH McKAY, No. 420 (S.C.) South Africa.

McLEOD, JAMES MORRISON, Past G. Sword Bearer, England, Sec. R.M.I. Boys.

MAIN, JOSEPH C., P.M., Secretary No. 157.

MAITLAND, PELHAM C., W.M. No. 2394, P.M. No. 1348.

MAKEPEACE, WALTER, P.M., Dist. G. Registrar, Eastern Archipelago.

MALCOLM, JOHN C., Past G. Deacon, England, Dep. Prov. G. Master, W. Yorks.

MALLETT, EDWARD, P.M. No. 141.

MANDER, JAMES, P.M., Treasurer, No. 1201.

MANFIELD, HARRY, P.M. No. 1911, P.P.G. Deacon, Norths and Hunts.

MANTELL, LOUIS, P.M. No. 1897.

MARTYN, Rev. CHARLES J., Past G. Chaplain, England.   (2 copies).

MARSH, J. HARDWICKE, P.M. No. 1730, Prov. G. Steward, W. Lancashire.

MASON, CHARLES LETCH, P.M., P.P.S.G.W. West Yorks.

MASON, JOHN, Past Grand Standard Bearer, England.   (2 copies).

MASON, J. J., Grand Secretary, Canada.

MASON, WILLIAM J., P.M. No. 1328, Vice-Pres. Board of General Purposes.   (2 copies).

MASSEY, HENRY, P.M. No. 619.

MATIER, CHARLES FITZGERALD, Past G. Standard Bearer, England, G. Sec. G. Lodge M.M.M.

MATTHEWS, JAMES H., Pres. Bd. Benevolence.

MATVEIEFF, BASIL, No. 176.

MAYER, DANIEL, W.M. No. 59.

MELVILLE, THOMAS SIDNEY, No. 1791.

MERCER, DAVID D., Past Grand Pursuivant, England.

MICKLEY, GEORGE, M.A., M.B., Past A.G.D. Ceremonies, England.

MIDDLEMIST, ROBERT P., P.M., Sec. No. 5, Past G. Steward, England.

MILLBOURN, ARTHUR E., D.C. No. 1237.

MILLS, WILLIAM G., P.M., Secretary No. 45.

MILNE, GEORGE G., Toronto.

MONEY-COUTTS, F. B., No. 1629.

MORBY, SAMUEL, P.M. No. 1853.

MORGAN, Alderman WALTER V., Past Grand Treasurer, England.

MORRIS, SPENCER W., P.M. No. 231, 1962, &c.

MOUTRAY, Rev. J. M., LL.D., Prov. G. Chaplain, Tyrone and Fermanagh.

MURRAY, Major J. D., Past G. Treasurer, England.

MURRAY, JAMES, P.M. No. 437, Scotland.

N

NAIRNE, PERCEVAL A., Past G. Deacon, England.

NAISH, ALFRED EDGAR, No. 2453.

NEWTON, JAMES, Prov G. Sec. East Lancashire.

NEWTON, JOHN, Past G. Pursuivant, England.   (2 copies.)

NEWTON, Lieut.-Col. WILLIAM, Dep. Prov. G.M. Notts, P.G. Deacon England.

NICHOLS, GEORGE, No. 360.

NICKERSON, SERENO D., Recording G. Secretary, Massachusetts.

NIXON, EDWARD JOHN, W.M. No. 2354, P.D.A.G. Std. Bearer, Transvaal.

NORRIS, EDWARD S., P.M. No. 32.

NUTTING, W. J., P.M. No. 231, 2469.

O

O'DUFFY, JOHN, Nos. 227, 232, 249, Ireland.

OHREN, MAGNUS, Past Assist. G.D. Ceremonies, England.

P

PALMER, JOHN S., P.M., Treas. No. 599, P.M. 1399, P.P.G. Warden, Oxon.

PARKHOUSE, SAMUEL H., P.M. Nos. 511, 1642.

PARSONS, H. W. SMITH, P.M. No. 804, P.P.G. Deacon, Hants and I. of Wight.

PARSONS, WILLIAM B., P.M. No. 2206.

PARTINGTON, CHARLES F., No. 3.

PEAT, WILLIAM THOMAS, P.M. No. 1656. Past Prov. G. Organist, Middlesex.

PECK, MICHAEL CHARLES, Prov. G. Sec. N. and E. Yorks, Past G. Standard Bearer, England.

PHILLIPS, EBENEZER S., St. John's No. 3, Connecticut.

PHIPOS, THOMAS JAMES, P.M. No. 1950.

PIERPOINT, EDWARD, P.M. No. 155, P.P.G. Warden, W. Lancashire

PINCKARD, GEORGE J., Rep. G.L. England, near the G.L. Louisiana.

PORCHER, HENRY, Secretary No. 1578.

POTTER, ROBERT F., P.M. No. 749, Prov. G. Tyler, Surrey.

POTTER, WALTER, P.M. No. 1260.

PRAEGER, Major HENRY J. F., No. 2484.

PRICE, BUN F., Past G. Master, Tennesse.

PRICE, F. COMPTON.

PRIOR, FREDERICK W., P.M. No. 90.

PRIOR, EPHRAIM, J.D. 1794, 2076.

PROBYN, Col. CLIFFORD, L.C.C., Grand Treasurer, England.

PROSSER, WALTER, No. 960.

PUCKLE, WALTER B., S.W. No. 162.

Q

QUARE, HORACE, P.M. No. 108.

QUICK, ALBERT CHARLES, P.M., Sec. No. 168.

R

RALLING, THOMAS J., Prov. G. Secretary Essex, Past A.G.D. of Ceremonies, England.

RAWLES, JAMES (late No. 507.)

RECKNELL, GEORGE S., W.M. No. 2466, P.M., Secretary No. 1728.

REDFORD, THOMAS, No. 1791.

REEP, J. ROBERTSON, P.M., Secretary No. 1260.

RICH, H. N., No. 9, British Columbia.

RICHARDSON, FRANK, Past G. Deacon, England.

RIDOUT, GEORGE, P.M. No. 1287.

ROBERTS, Rev. CHARLES E., M.A., Prov. G. Chaplain, Bucks.

ROBERTSON, JOHN ROSS, Past G. Master, Canada.

ROBINSON, FRANCIS W., P.M. No. 704.

ROBINSON, FRANCIS, W.M. No. 42 (I.C.), Dep. Prov. G. Secretary, Antrim.

ROBINSON, JOHN, P.M. No. 106, 128 (I.C.), Past Prov. S.G. Deacon, Antrim. (2 copies.)

ROSE, GEORGE W., J.W. No. 1271, Organist No. 632.

ROSE, HENRY R., Past G Organist, England.

ROUMIEU, REGINALD ST A., Past G. Supt. of Works, England.

ROWLAND, JAMES, No. 2343.

RYLAND, FRED. C., No. 74.

RYLANDS, W. HARRY, P.M. Nos. 2, 2076, Past A.G.D. of Ceremonies, England. (2 copies.)

S

SAUNDERS, W. H. J., P.M. No. 139. Michigan.

SCURRAH, W. ALFRED, P.M. No. 1674, &c., Past Grand Standard Bearer, England. (2 copies.)

SETON, SIR BRUCE M., Bart., Past G. Deacon, England.

SHERWIN, HENRY H., P.M. No. 420. P.P.G. Supt. of Works Bucks.

SHERWOOD, N. N., P.M., Treasurer No. 231.

SIMCOX, JOSEPH, P.M. No. 1501, P.P.G. Organist, Bucks.

SLYMAN, JOHN, P.M. No. 1730, P.P.G. Deacon West Lancashire.

SMITH, JOHN, W.M. No. 2490.

SMITH, GENERAL J. C., Past G. Master, Rep. of G.L. England at G.L. of Illinois.

SMITHETT, WILLIAM, Past G. Deacon, England.

SMYTH, HUGH, P.M. No. 121 (I.C.), P.P.G.L.O. Antrim.

SMYTHE, ALFRED, J.P., P.M. No. 269 (I.C.), Rep G.L. New Brunswick at G.L. Ireland.

SNELL, BENJAMIN, M.A., P.M. No. 709.

SPELLER, JAMES, P.M. No. 1677, Past Prov. G. Deacon, Essex. (12 copies.)

SPETH, GEORGE WILLIAM, Past A.G.D. Ceremonies, England.

SPILLING, HENRY G., No. 2148.

SPILLING, WALTER F., No. 435.

SQUIRES, JAMES W., P.M., Chippewa Falls, Wisconsin.

STEGGLES, RICHARD W., P.M. No. 2502.

STENNING, ALEXANDER R., Past G. Sup. Works, England.

STEPHENS, JAMES, Past Dep. G.D. Ceremonies, England.

STEVENSON, GEORGE D., P.M. No. 2148, P.P.G. Purst. Kent.

STEVENSON, JAMES H., J.D. No. 2148.

STILES, WILLIAM MASON, Past G. Treasurer, England.

STIMSON, EDWARD, P.M., Treasurer No. 15.

STRACHAN, JOHN, Q.C., Grand Registrar, England.

STRONG, Alderman T. VEZEY, W.M. Elect, No. 1538.

SUDLOW, ROBERT CLAY, Past G. Stand. Bearer, England.

SUIRDALE, Viscount, No. 1629.

SUTHERLAND, HENRY, M.D., W.M. G. Stewards' Lodge, Past G. Deacon, England.

SUTTIE, DAVID A., No. 357, Michigan.

SUTTON, EDWARD B., J.P., Past G. Deacon, England.　(4 copies.)

SWINDEN, F. G., Prov. G. Secretary, Warwickshire.

SWEET, JOHN T., No. 1632, I.G. No. 2694.

T

TATE, Dr. W. B., Past P.S.G.W., Nottinghamshire.

TAYLOR, ALEX. JOHN, P.M. No. 1791.

TAYLOR, JAMES K. (late 1897).

TAYLOR, ROBERT, P.M. No. 2148.

TAYLOR, W. CAMPBELL, P.M., Secretary No. 913.

TERNAN, Dr. O., P.P.S.G. Warden, Prov. G. Sec., Tyrone & Fermanagh.

TERRY, JAMES, Past G. Sword Bearer, Eng., Sec. R.M.B. Institution. (2 copies.)

THOMAS, JOHN JOSEPH, Past G. Standard Bearer, England.

THORPE, CHARLES E., P.M. No. 360.

THORP, JOHN T., P.M., P.P.S.G. Warden, Leicestershire.

TOBIAS, HENRY A., P.M. Nos. 59, 1017, 1502, P.P.G. Supt. of Works, W. Lancashire.

TOWNEND, HARRY, W.M. No. 2265.

TREVOR, TUDOR, P.M. Nos. 41, 2069, P.P.G.D.C., West Yorks.

TREWINNARD, ALFRED H., P.M. No. 228, 1693, Sec. No. 1950.

TROLLOPE, THOMAS, M.D., Past. G. Deacon, England.

V

VALLENTINE, SAMUEL, P.M. No. 9, Past G. Pursuivant, England.

VASSAR-SMITH, R. V., Dep. Prov. G.M. Gloucestershire, Past G. Deacon, England.

VENABLES, ROWLAND GEORGE, Dep. Prov. G.M. Shropshire, P.A.G. Director of Ceremonies, England.

VINCENT, WILLIAM, P.P.G. Std. Br. Middlesex, Past G. Std. Bearer. England.

W

WAKEFORD, GEORGE W., P.M. No. 1, Past Dep. G. Master, Prince Edward Island.

WALFORD, ERNEST L., P.M. No. 2148, P.P.A.G. Sec. Kent.

WALLACE. Lieut.-Col. ROBERT H., P.M., Past P.S.G. Warden, Down, Ireland.

WALLS, Major T. C., Past G. Standard Bearer, England.

WARD, HORATIO, P.P.G.W., Kent, &c., Past Dep. G. Swd. Br., England.

WARRINGTON, Richard S., Past G. Steward, England.

WARVELLE, GEORGE W., P.M., Chicago.

WATSON, JAMES PROCTOR, J.P., Nos. 944, 2581.

WATSON, WILLIAM, P.P.S.G. Warden, Hon. Librarian, W. Yorks.

WATTS, GEORGE NELSON, P.M. No. 194.

WEBB, CHARLES H., P.M., Sec. No. 174, 1607.

WEBB, JOHN D., W.M. No. 1314, S.W. 1745.

WEBSTER. SIR AUGUSTUS. Bart., Past G. Deacon. England.

WEINEL, FREDERICK P., P.M. No. 1828, J.D. No. 1745.

WELDON, J. H., P.M. and Secretary No. 49, Ireland.

WELLER-POLEY, THOMAS, Past G. Deacon, England.

WELSFORD, W. OAKLEY, P.M. No. 1321.

WHITEMAN, JOHN, No. 87.

WHYTEHEAD. THOMAS B., P.P.S.G.W. N. and E. Yorks, Past G. Sword Bearer, England.

WIEBE, CARL C., Grand Master, Hamburg.

WILCOX, C. A., P.M. No. 659, Illinois.

WILKINS, FREDERICK J.. S.W. No. 338, Scotland.

WILLIAMS. EDMUND NELSON G., P.P.G. Chaplain, Norfolk.

WILLIAMS, ERNEST, S.W. No. 1271, J.D. No. 632.

WILLIAMS, S. STACKER, Past Grand Master, Ohio.

WILLIAMS, THOMAS, No. 2278.

WILLING, JAMES, P.M. Nos. 177, 1507, 1744, 1987, 2455, &c.   (2 copies.)

WILLS, THOMAS HENRY, P.M. No. 1402.

WILSON, PEREGRINE O., W.M. No. 2315.

WITHEY, THOMAS ARCHER, P.M. No. 1299, P.P.G. Registrar, W. Lancs.

WRIGHT, Rev. C. E. L., P.P.G. Chaplain N. and E. Yorks, Past G. Chaplain, Egypt.

WYATT, Rev. VITRUVIUS P., P.M. No. 2343, P.P.G. Chaplain, Bucks.

WYLIE, ROBERT, Dep. Prov. G. Master, West Lancashire.

Kirby Lodge of Instruction, No. 263.

GEORGE RANKIN, No. 1641, Preceptor.

BAKER, WILLIAM, S.W. No. 2205, Secretary.

BARNARD, ARTHUR M., P.M. No. 1964.

CHANDLER, ROBERT S., S.W. No. 2700, Steward No. 1962

COOK, LEONARD G., I.G. No. 1194.

CORP, JAMES, P.M. No. 2148.

DAVIES, THOMAS W., No. 1965.

FITZGERALD, J. V. VESEY, Q.C., P.M. No. 502, P.P.S.G.W. Warwickshire.

HARRIS, ARTHUR F., J.W. No. 2148.

HUMPHRIES, HENRY, S.D. No. 569.

JEFFERY, THOMAS GEORGE, W.M. No. 2148.

LANG, THOMAS K., No. 784.

LANGLIN, V. CODINA, I.G. No. 2458.

LEIGHTON, ALBERT, S.W. No. 263.

LEWIS, CHARLES, P.M. 1703, 2508, P.P.G. Deacon, Essex.

LYON, H. THOMSON, P.M. No. 2563.

MARTIN, JOHN, No. 1056.

PRITCHARD, HENRY, P.M. & Sec. No. 263, P.P.G Treas. Middlesex.

QUILTER, JOSEPH R., No. 2427.

RAYNER, GEORGE H., No. 1965.

ROWLEY, WILLIAM, P.M. Nos. 1924, 2148, S.W. No. 854, Ireland.

RUSHTON, F. T., P.M. 8, Past G. Steward, England.

SMITH, Major ALLAN, P.M. Nos. 355, 702, Scotland, P.J.G. Warden, All Scottish Freemasonry in India.

SUDLOW, ROBERT CLAY, Past G. Standard Bearer, England.

TIDMARSH, JOHN, P.M. No. 2157, 2163, P.P.G.D. Middlesex.

WARD, HORATIO, Past Dep. G. Sword Bearer, England.

WARD, FRANK W., No. 31, Secretary No. 2508, Secretary.

WATTS, HENRY, J.W. No. 108, Steward No. 1479.

WELLCOME, HENRY S., P.M. Nos. 3 & 2397, Treasurer.

WEST, DAVID D., P.M. No. 108.

Star Lodge of Instruction, No. 1275.

WALTER MARTIN, P.M. No. 879, Past A.G. Purst. England,
Preceptor.

ALMOND, JOHN, W.M. No. 2500.

BARBER, RICHARD W., W.M. No. 198.

BARSON, GEORGE, S.W. No. 1669.

BLANCHARD, GEORGE C., P.M. No. 1275, Secretary.

BUGLER, THOMAS, P.M. No. 1155.

BUNTING, WALTER S., W.M. Elect 2318, Sec. 2500.

BURGESS, THOMAS J., J.D. No. 45.

EAMES, ROBERT H., No. 2500.

ELLINGER, JOHN, P.M., Sec. No. 2222.

GRAY, PERCY, No. 1597.

HARPER, HAROLD J., P.M. No. 879.

HAWKINS, GEORGE, No. 198.

KIPPS, WILLIAM, P.M., P.P.G Org. Kent, &c.

NIGHTINGALE, EDWARD W., P.M. Sec. No. 87, 879, &c.

PALMER, HENRY, No. 65.

POINTON, JOSEPH S., W.M. Elect, No. 1861, J.W. No. 1901.

ROBINSON, FREDERICK, J.W. No. 1309.

SIMMONS, WILLIAM G., P.M. No. 1155.

SYKES, WALTER, P.M. No. 1597, P.A.G.D.C. Middlesex.

WATERMAN, GEORGE. P.M. No. 147.

WHALLEY, LAWRENCE J. DE, *B.Sc.* No. 1275.

WILKINSON, JOSEPH D., P.M., Secretary No. 879.

WITTY, JOHN HENRY, *F.R.H.S.*, No. 1155.

Earl of Clarendon Lodge of Instruction, No. 1984.

JOHN P. TAYLOR, P.M. No. 1894, Assist. Prov. G.D.C. Herts,
Preceptor.

ASHBY, EDWIN, No. 1984.

CAMP, HARRY, No. 1743.

FELTON, WILLIAM, No. 1549.

GREEN, JAMES T., No. 1757.

GRIGG, WILLIAM, No. 1984.

HALSEY, CHARLES H., J.W. No. 1984.

HINGLEY, JOHN H., S.D. No. 2218.

HORTON, HENRY, S.D. No. 1984.

JAMES, WILLIAM J., W.M. No. 2218.

JUDGE, WILLIAM, I.G. No. 1984.

SOUTHAM, JOSEPH, P.M. No. 1984, Treasurer.

SPENCER, EDWARD J., J.W. No. 2218.

STARK, EDWARD, J.D. No. 1984.

OXLEY, EDWARD C. RICE, W.M. No. 2128.

THOM, CHARLES, Montrose Kilwinning, No. 15, Scotland.

VEAL, CHARLES J., P.M. No. 1549.

HISTORICAL MASONIC WORKS

BY

HENRY SADLER.

"𝕸asonic 𝕱acts and 𝕱ictions," 1887 (*out of print*).

𝕹otes on the
Ceremony of 𝕴nstallation.

OPINIONS OF THE MASONIC PRESS.

" We consider Bro. SADLER has fully made out his case, and that he merits the thanks of the brethren generally for the important service he has thus rendered. *   *   *   *   *   *   *   *   *   * These anecdotes are very interesting, and will greatly edify the Craft, but they would have been better in a more subordinate position.   Except as regards this trifling blemish, Bro. SADLER has succeeded admirably, and the book has the further merit of being clearly printed, neatly bound, and embellished with a portrait and short biographical notice of Bro. SIR ALBERT WOODS, to whom, indeed, it is dedicated."—*The Freemason.* London.

" The book throughout is of an interesting character, showing a part of the work done by the Craft in days gone by, and introducing the reader to most of those who took a prominent share in its affairs." *The Freemasons' Chronicle,* London.

" It is an interesting little volume, showing that there is an authorised Ceremony of Installation dating back to 1723, how it was sanctioned, and what, in outline, it is."—*The Keystone,* Philadelphia.

In Demy 8vo., Cloth Boards.   *Price 2s. 6d.*

GEORGE KENNING,

16 AND 16A, GREAT QUEEN STREET, LONDON, W.C.

THOMAS DUNCKERLEY,

His Life, Labours, and Letters,

Including some Masonic and Naval Memorials of the Eighteenth Century,

WITH A PREFACE BY

WILLIAM HARRY RYLANDS, Esq., F.S.A.

THIS Work contains numerous Letters, Extracts, &c., relating to Masonry in Bristol, Dorsetshire, Essex, Gloucestershire, Hampshire, Herefordshire, The Isle of Wight, Somerset and Wiltshire, of which Counties DUNCKERLEY was Prov. Grand Master; also Portraits, reproduced by the autotype process, from rare mezzotint engravings in the British Museum of :—

His Majesty King George II. of England; Dunckerley's reputed father.

H.R.H. Frederick Lewis, Prince of Wales, son of the above; the First of the Royal Family who was made a Freemason.

Thomas Dunckerley in Masonic regalia, with facsimile of his autograph, Book-plate, Seals, &c.

PRESS NOTICES.

"There can be but one opinion as to the third work which has emanated from the pen of Bro. SADLER. As regards himself, it very materially enhances his reputation as an author, while, as regards the subject of his memoir, it places before us a fund of information which enables us to form a clearer and more complete idea than has hitherto been possible of the part played by Dunckerley in the several branches of Masonry existent in his day."—*The Freemason*, London.

I consider that my friend SADLER's *Life of Thomas Dunckerley* is one of the most original, valuable and interesting contributions made to Masonic literature during this century, and well deserves the success it has obtained."—WILLIAM JAMES HUGHAN, P.G.D.

"As a history of Freemasonry in the 18th century, the book will be found of considerable value to all connected with the Order, and it should find many readers in the West of England."—*Western Morning News*.

340 Pages Demy Octavo, handsomely bound in cloth gilt, bevelled boards, red edges.

PRICE 7s. 6d.

GEORGE KENNING,

16 AND 16A, GREAT QUEEN STREET, LONDON, W.C.

CPSIA information can be obtained at www.ICGtesting.com
Printed in the USA
BVOW052312180112

280901BV00003B/5/A